THE
KINGDOM
MIND

FINDING TREASURE IN
THE THOUGHTS OF GOD

HOWARD TILLMAN

urbanpress

The Kingdom Mind
by Howard Tillman
Copyright © 2018 Howard Tillman

ISBN # 978-1-63360-090-4

For Worldwide Distribution Printed in the U.S.A.

Urban Press
P.O. Box 8881
Pittsburgh, PA 15221-0881 USA
412.646.2780

www.urbanpress.us

CONTENTS

INTRODUCTION

It has been my privilege to pastor a local church now for 28 years. Before that, I traveled in ministry as an evangelist and then founded and led my own ministry. While I have not seen all there is to see in the church world, I have seen a lot and I am at the point in my life where I can speak from an abundance of experience. I don't know if that makes me wise, but I am certainly wiser than I was when I started. If I can share what I have learned to help an existing or future leader, then I am always happy to do that.

In my church, I've recently been addressing our need to have our youth become an integral part of what we are doing instead of having them watch everyone else. If we don't do that, our church will quickly get "old" in our thinking and our behavior, and we will become increasingly irrelevant. To include this next generation, we cannot simply adopt new programs; we must change our ministry philosophy.

This has required that I stress training and development while at the same time putting more emphasis on outreach to youth and building the church from within so it can be relevant when it ventures into the community. We are using new outreach techniques to share the gospel, while engaging our members and those in attendance to help them utilize their creative talents. It has not been easy.

Years ago, I began to look at ministry as an opportunity to tap into the genius of an individual. We as leaders often don't consider the value of the people as it relates to God's kingdom. We only think of their value to our organization, which for pastors is the church. When we do that – only seeing how they can help our church grow – those people go outside the church to find ways to express their genius – and by genius, I mean purpose, gifts, talents, and interests. They attend church, but they don't give the best of who they are to the church. Their best often goes someplace else.

We are not confronting young people and new members with questions like: With the creative genius inside you, how can you use that genius to help build God's kingdom? How can you influence or impact your generation with that creative genius? How can you impact the lives of other people?

We as church leaders have not equipped our people to use enough of their creative genius to make a difference in the kingdom of God, and that should be our primary purpose. What I am describing is what Paul wrote about in Ephesians 4:11-13:

> So Christ himself gave the apostles, the prophets, the evangelists, the pastors, and teachers, to equip his people for works of service, so that the body of Christ may be built up until we all reach unity in the faith and in the knowledge of the Son of God and become mature, attaining to the whole measure of the fullness of Christ.

Today people are bombarded with many options and diversions. The church is no longer the main or only act in the community. There are many people who say they have done the church thing a long time and they are tired and burned out. It's become like a job, and therefore they want to retire from being an active Christian, content to live out their days as church attenders and not Kingdom builders. From my vantage point, I'm not sensing a good vibe at all.

This approach to Christianity is not consistent with the biblical role for a believer. The Holy Spirit does not go on a sabbatical. He continuously lives in us, leading and guiding us into all truth and into ventures that will bring the gospel to the people who without us, do not have a chance to experience Jesus Christ. The mission never goes away for anyone who has put their faith in Christ.

No matter how exhilarating and exciting a person's job or career is, and regardless of how much of their talent and creativity they use or get paid to express, they are not using their genius to further God's kingdom. On their job, they have a limited impact but they could have a worldwide impact if we help them find a way to contribute their genius to the spread of God's kingdom, which is what Jesus commanded us to do:

> "Therefore go and make disciples of all nations, baptizing them in the name of the Father and of the Son and of the Holy Spirit, and teaching them to obey everything I have commanded you. And surely I am with you always, to the very end of the age" (Matthew 28:19-20).

My current emphasis on transformation, to what I will refer to as *The Kingdom Mind* in this book, is challenging us to innovate because the model of church, as most people know it, does not lend itself to what we are trying to do. The current model involves attending church on certain days, contributing to its upkeep, participating in whatever ministries may be relevant to our or our family's needs, and then going home.

We attend and are inspired, but then we go right back to what we were doing in our work or our neighborhood because we have not understood what we can do after the excitement and inspiration of church are over. We must create a new church model that people can understand and relate to, so they can determine where in the model they can invest their lives. That will require a *Kingdom Mind* both to create and also to participate.

In these uncertain times, we need to be more focused on the kingdom of God. That truth is not directed to a specific age group or race. It's a challenge to believers, especially to leaders, that we need to shift our thinking where the Church and the Kingdom are concerned. We need to have less church allegiance and much more Kingdom allegiance.

In this book, I will talk about what it will require from leaders to lead this new revolution, perhaps better termed a reformation, in modern church work and life. For this reformation to occur, we need *The Kingdom Mind* that is focused on and shaped by what Jesus and the Bible say about the kingdom of God. If we as leaders don't change our thinking and approach to ministry, then we will keep going down the same path we are currently on, and I am concerned for the body of Christ if that happens. John Maxwell has stated that everything rises and falls with leadership, and I agree with that statement.

I am going to share with you my own *Kingdom Mind* that has brought me to where I am today. I will present this book in four sections: Love God; Love the Vision; Love the People; and Love the Work. In all four sections, I will outline the specific Kingdom thinking that must take place for change and reformation to occur. We will season each section with a generous helping of biblical examples and principles, mostly but not exclusively from the life of Moses from Exodus in the Old Testament.

There is a danger whenever leaders come out with a new thought or strategy. Everyone will scrutinize those leaders to see how they are applying that concept in their own sphere. I currently pastor New Covenant Believers' Church in Columbus, Ohio and have also co-founded a movement labeled Kingdom Brand Development Ministries (KBDM). If you come to study either entity, you will recognize some of the things I describe in this book, but you will also see that both are a work in progress.

I am still learning and growing in my ability to lead

because society and culture are constantly shifting and changing as well. It's almost like a video game that unfolds as we go. As soon as we finish one level, we graduate to a new, more complicated and challenging level. That is how I feel as a leader today, but that does not exempt me from playing the game. Many of my peers seem content to master one level without moving on to the next. I refuse to be like them.

At the end of the book, I will describe KBDM and will invite you to consider being part of what we are doing as a network of churches. It is a true network and not a formal entity of bishops or churches, or a denomination. It is a group of leaders and future leaders who are willing to seek *The Kingdom Mind* and then walk out that *Mind* as they lead their churches. Whether you align with our network or not is irrelevant, but I do hope and pray that will align with our concepts, for there is much work to be done for the kingdom of God. That will require a group of leaders committed to the uncertainty of trying new concepts as we attempt to make the church relevant in this day and hour.

Bishop Howard Tillman
Columbus, Ohio
June 2018

SECTION ONE
LOVE GOD

CHAPTER 1
WHY ARE WE DOING WHAT WE DO?

It may seem strange that I start a book about a new approach to leadership thinking with something as basic as "Love God." You may already be a leader who has devoted your entire adult life to church work and growth. You have faithfully preached, taught, earned theological degrees, and contributed to and participated in missions work. It would seem it is a "given" that you love God.

I am not writing to dispute or question your love for God, but I know from experience that there are many rivals in ministry to love for God, and those rivals can sometimes subtly supplant our love for God as the first priority. Sometimes we fall in love with our gifts, talents, and abilities. Others fall in love with the position, power, and prestige that leadership brings in some church settings. Still others love their church for what it once was or what it meant to their family or race, and are emotionally attached to that memory.

The first church Jesus addressed in the book of Revelation had the problem of being good at what they did:

To the angel of the church in Ephesus write:

These are the words of him who holds the seven stars in his right hand and walks among the seven golden lampstands. I know your deeds, your hard work and your perseverance. I know that you cannot tolerate wicked people, that you have tested those who claim to be apostles but are not, and have found them false. You have persevered and have endured hardships for my name, and have not grown weary.

Yet I hold this against you: You have forsaken the love you had at first. Consider how far you have fallen! Repent and do the things you did at first. If you do not repent, I will come to you and remove your lampstand from its place. But you have this in your favor: You hate the practices of the Nicolaitans, which I also hate.

Whoever has ears, let them hear what the Spirit says to the churches. To the one who is victorious, I will give the right to eat from the tree of life, which is in the paradise of God (Revelation 2:1-7).

The church in Ephesus had abandoned its first love even though it had a distinguished record as a strong and steadfast church. They started out doing things for God, and they continued doing those things, but someplace along the way, they started doing them for other reasons. They became professionals at conducting the work of the church. Jesus directed them to get back to the first things, and those first things were all summarized by the phrase "loving God." *The Kingdom Mind* is built, developed, and nurtured on a love for God and His word.

What I do in ministry, or what anyone does for that matter, must emanate from a love for Jesus Christ. We must say to ourselves that our job is to carry out His will for His church, and not the will of the people, the denomination, or the prevailing culture. We can't be people who simply attend or work for a church. We must get over what I refer to as the pew mentality of ministry, where to some extent we entertain or want to be entertained.

A PURPOSE FOR MEETING

As leaders, we must ask what we want to produce in people's lives when we deliver our messages from the pulpit or lead a deacon's or elder's meeting. Are we simply having church, or is there a purpose to what we do? Are we meeting together on the third Tuesday of every month because that's what we have always done, or are we meeting to discuss how to advance the Kingdom through our church work? Paul had a purpose when he planted a new church comprised of Christ's disciples, which he described in Colossians 1:28-29:

> He [Christ] is the one we proclaim, admonishing and teaching everyone with all wisdom, so that we may present everyone fully mature in Christ. To this end I strenuously contend with all the energy Christ so powerfully works in me.

When we hear a message, we should ask why we are being given this message. We must personalize and also ask: What am I supposed to do with this message? With whom am I supposed to share this message? Too often we hear messages and evaluate the delivery of the message, sometimes overlooking the lack of content because the preaching style was our preferred style. That does not produce *The Kingdom Mind*, but rather a church mind. We are content to have had church, to experience church, and then to evaluate church ("We had *church* today!" or "The music wasn't anointed today").

We sponsor big events to grow churches and we build event ministries. Those event-based initiatives may be emotionally-charged and inspirational, designed to touch people's hearts, but they can be short-lived and don't create a Kingdom lifestyle. Christianity is not a job, it's a lifestyle. If it's a lifestyle, then Christian behavior is the norm, not church attendance or denominational allegiance.

If leaders and followers respond properly, we don't have an

attitude that we *must* get up to pray or read our Bibles. Those practices become an integral part of who we are. They must become normative behaviors that our special events help maintain instead of replacing. We all know people who are good church goers but then leave church not living up to what they learned. That is because they have a church mind instead of *The Kingdom Mind*.

As leaders and disciples, our life goal is to be people of influence. Whatever we do, we do it all because we love Him, not the gifts or opportunities to express the gifts He gave us. What should move us to action is who Jesus is and what He's done for us. In other words, we are motivated by our love for God. Then we pass that love along to the people who follow, who sit and listen and then respond to our messages.

Those people become people of influence who may or may not be seen by the masses, but in the sphere where they function, they become known. They are known by the people in their department at the job, or in the classroom at school. They influence their teammates or the members of their garden club. They will be known as people of influence because church leaders they follow knew how to influence them rather than control them.

I discussed our need to engage people's genius in the Introduction. If we as leaders don't do that, people go to work and don't understand how their work serves to extend God's kingdom. They are only working to pursue raises, promotions, or to have a place to get away from their problems at home. That is not part of *The Kingdom Mind*. They must learn to be at their jobs because they love God first and foremost, and while they are there, they must be His representatives and ambassadors, reaching and influencing people whom the Church cannot reach.

OUR STAGE

The Lord assigns each of us what I call a stage on which to perform, whether we want one or not. Shakespeare wrote a famous quote about the concept of the stage: "All the world's a stage, and all the men and women merely players; they have their exits and their entrances." We are not followers of Shakespeare but of Christ who referred to our stage as our encounters with those who are outside of God's kingdom:

> "You are the light of the world. A town built on a hill cannot be hidden. Neither do people light a lamp and put it under a bowl. Instead they put it on its stand, and it gives light to everyone in the house. In the same way, let your light shine before others, that they may see your good deeds and glorify your Father in heaven" (Matthew 5:14-16).

When we get on public transportation, that's a stage. When we go to work, that's a stage. When we go to the supermarket, that's a stage. When we go to the park with our families, that's a stage. When we go to soccer practice or a game with our children, that's a stage. Every day we have chances to make an impact on somebody who sees us on that stage.

Jesus didn't say that the only stage was the church. He said that there would be many stages from which our lights may shine. For most people, their stage is not what goes on within the four walls of the church because that's the place where they learn, get information, and receive inspiration and motivation to perform on their stage. Our job as leaders is to prepare the people to shine, but we must do that not first and foremost because we love the people (we will discuss that in Section Three), but because we love Him.

Let's be honest. If you are reading this, you know how church should be done. If you lead or follow, you know what time it should start, how long it should go, how the music should sound, and what is required of the various role players. If one of those players is out for a week or longer, someone knows how to step in and fill that gap.

My point is that we are having church, but do we know *why* we are having it? What is the end result we are trying to produce in the people? If we have lost track of that, if we meet only to collect the money and keep the people from going to another church, then we have lost our first love and must renew our love for God before we can be personally renewed or facilitate renewal among the people. We must understand that church is simply one stage, perhaps for some the most important stage, but not the *only* stage.

BIG ISLAND, LITTLE ISLAND

Recently I taught the church from 1 Peter 2:1-3:

Therefore, rid yourselves of all malice and all deceit, hypocrisy, envy, and slander of every kind. Like newborn babies, crave pure spiritual milk, so that by it you may grow up in your salvation, now that you have tasted that the Lord is good.

Peter instructed his readers to rid themselves of malice, slander, and envy. Peter expected them to act a certain way because they were born again. It occurred to me that we have the physical house of God, which I refer to as the big island, where people come to be refreshed, motivated, and inspired, as well as to learn and gain Kingdom information that will lead to *The Kingdom Mind* and Kingdom formation. All that will assist them in their daily lives.

If our goal is only to have church, which we know how to do, and then the people go home and act the same way they have always acted, we have stopped loving God and we are then loving church. We have become like the Ephesian church described in Revelation.

Peter went on to teach that we are interconnected to and interdependent with one another. When we come together, we bring hope and light to each other. When we do that, then we are taking full advantage of our big-island gatherings. Otherwise, we are just having meetings, the effects of which won't last very long on the little islands that people go home to. When that happens, people get tired and fall away, instead of leaving to go influence the world because they have been influenced by one another – and the Spirit of the Lord.

Our gatherings have a purpose and that is to prepare

those present to go back on stage. They can leave the big island and go back to their little islands and be people of influence there. When the big island becomes entertainment, does not hold its constituency accountable, or does not give those attending the tools they need for their marriages, relationship with their children, or to thrive in their vocation, then we have failed to live up to the expectations and possibilities of what the church, the big island, was meant to be.

When we don't give them the tools, we are not meeting their needs to serve the kingdom of God on the stage where God has placed them. When we do that effectively, the people of God have an enthusiasm about what is happening on the big island because it has helped their marriages and families, their finances, and their careers. Then they go to their little islands and talk about their big island.

As we continue the outdated ways of doing church, we often employ antiquated approaches to evangelism. They don't work like they used to because it's a different time and era. People are looking for church folk and leaders who are authentic, committed, and honest. There are people looking for disciples of Jesus who live what they say they believe. Authentic believers influence others and those influenced people then take the gospel to their stage.

The church cannot be a place of entertainment or ethnic identify. The people in the pews needs to know we are *all* here to learn from one another (not just the pastor) and to empower each other. That approach to ministry excites me because that is what God intended the church to be and do.

But alas, I am getting ahead of myself. We must first exhaust our discussion of loving God and returning to our first works. Since this book is a discussion of *The Kingdom Mind*, it would be good to take a step back and examine the key word in that two-word phrase and that word is Kingdom. Let's take a look at the concept of the kingdom of God in the next chapter.

KINGDOM MIND THOUGHTS

1. We know how to "do" church, but what is the goal of our gatherings? What do you expect from church when you attend?

2. Everyone has a stage on which God wants them to act out in full view of others, including you. Can you list your stages?

3. That stage for a few is the church but for most people, it is out in the "world."

4. We as leaders must equip people to influence others in their world.

CHAPTER 2
THE KINGDOM

What I am labeling *The Kingdom Mind* was introduced when Jesus was meeting with His disciples and they asked Him to teach them to pray. Here is His response:

> Now it came to pass, as He was praying in a certain place, when He ceased, *that* one of His disciples said to Him, "Lord, teach us to pray, as John also taught his disciples." So He said to them, "When you pray, say: Our Father in heaven, Hallowed be Your name. Your kingdom come, your will be done on earth as *it is* in heaven. Give us day by day our daily bread. And forgive us our sins, for we also forgive everyone who is indebted to us. And do not lead us into temptation, but deliver us from the evil one" (Luke 11:1-4 NKJV).

Jesus provided the guidelines for our prayers, but the key phrase I want to focus on is "your kingdom come, your will be done on earth as it is in heaven." When people understand God wants them to carry out His will here on earth just like it is carried out in heaven, they have a life changing revelation. We say that those people have seen the Kingdom and they are never the same.

When Jesus' earthly ministry began, He did not begin to build the Church, but proclaimed that the Kingdom was at hand:

> Now after John was put in prison, Jesus came to Galilee, preaching the gospel of the kingdom of God, and saying, "The time is fulfilled, and the kingdom of God is at hand. Repent, and believe in the gospel" (Mark 1:14-15).

Later when talking with Nicodemus and answering his questions, Jesus made this statement: "Most assuredly, I say to you, unless one is born again, he cannot see the kingdom of God" (John 3:3). Nicodemus was confused by Jesus' answer and responded, "How can a man be born when he is old? Can he enter a second time into his mother's womb and be born?" (John 3:4), to which Jesus replied, "Most assuredly, I say to you, unless one is born of water and the Spirit, he cannot enter the kingdom of God. That which is born of the flesh is flesh, and that which is born of the Spirit is spirit" (John 3:5-6).

Jesus did not talk to Nicodemus about belonging to a synagogue and He did not explain the concept of the church-yet-to-come. Jesus talked about the Kingdom. In fact, Jesus was an embodiment of the Kingdom He announced and proclaimed, for He perfectly carried out the Father's will. Jesus did not just proclaim that the Kingdom was here, He modeled what the Kingdom of God on earth should look like.

It makes an interesting study to put the word "kingdom" into a Bible search engine and see all the verses that come up in the gospels and epistles. Then put "church" in the same engine and it is clear that the early followers of Jesus discussed the Kingdom much more often than they did the church.

WHAT IS THE KINGDOM?

The kingdom of God is simply a term that summarizes

God's reign, rule, and government for His servants here on earth. The Kingdom is not something to be discussed or studied unless those efforts lead to submitting to the requirements of the Kingdom. Therefore, it is possible for someone to come to a salvation experience but not submit to the requirements of the Kingdom, still living a self-willed, carnal lifestyle.

Grace is absolutely essential in the process and operation of the Kingdom because grace is God doing for us what we cannot do for ourselves by His favor and enablement. This is for His glory so that we can be and do what we cannot be and do by ourselves. If we live under the reign, rule, and government of God, and submit ourselves to that, then the grace of God functions on our behalf, helping, guiding, energizing, and motivating us through the Holy Spirit so that we can implement and carry out the will of the Father on the earth.

Our minds then must be transformed so that we can function accordingly. We need to receive information that will enable us to do the things necessary to live in the Kingdom. Since the Kingdom is the reign, rule, and government of God, we need to ask what that will look like on earth. What does it look like in leadership? What does it look like in terms of our interaction with and functioning in the body of Christ? It is essential that we have *The Kingdom Mind* if we are to properly and accurately represent Him on the stages we have been assigned.

I was reflecting on the Kingdom recently and it dawned on me that we must have faith to live according to the Kingdom. When we have faith, we cannot compartmentalize our service on earth to just our spiritual gift, regardless of whether it is the gift of preaching, leadership, singing, or whatever gift it is that we have been given. We must also understand that there is a morality and an ethical standard that must be connected to that gift. What do I mean by this?

You should accept if you are called into the Kingdom that your gift is not to be used as you see fit. God may want you to express your gift in or outside the church. You need a Kingdom mindset that comes from God's grace to grasp that you don't just give your life to Christ and then move on with business as usual. You don't just go to church and then spend the other 165 hours in the week pursuing your dreams or plans. Your gift is not given to enrich you but to enrich and empower others, both inside and outside the church.

Our lives must manifest Jesus' teaching and His thoughts, His doctrine, ideas, and the reality of His resurrected being. How can we do that? We will not only pray "your will be done on earth as it is in heaven," but after we pray, we will be part of making it a reality. We can do God's will here just like His ministering servants the angels do in heaven, but we don't have to wait till we get there to do it.

What does it look like when we live under the rule of God's government? First, our lives take on the spirit of the Great Commission that commands us to go into all the world. Once we accept that Commission, we must learn how to implement that Commission into our day-to-day lives.

Our church supports missionaries in Venezuela, India, and in Africa. We send our money to those people who are making an impact in those places and we share in their impact. When Jesus said go into all the world, He also meant cities like Columbus, into specific streets like Upper Arlington and Westerville. As we go, we represent the government of God and extend the reign and rule of God in those areas. That's part of what it means to have *The Kingdom Mind*.

THE KINGDOM MIND IN CHURCH

Once again, my definition of Kingdom is that people are under the reign, rule, and government of God. We pray, "Our father who art in heaven, hallowed be your name. Your **kingdom** come, your will be done on earth as it is in heaven. Lord, we want Your will on earth as Your will is in done in Heaven. We know Your will is for us to go. Your will is for us to preach the gospel and make disciples." Once we pray it, then we must go do it.

That's a different mentality because some people believe a church must have a media presence on TV if it is going to grow. When we start thinking like that, we can actually bypass our Kingdom responsibility. When we use the media to market our message, nine times out of ten our audience is already Christian. We have the best opportunity to reach those who are not Christians by equipping those who are sitting there in the pews to go reach them.

This thinking about church and those who attend requires a change of heart. Pastors must understand what motivates them to do what they do. They must ask, "Am I pursuing something because it's a good idea or is it a personal and leadership value?" Empowering people is not a program for me; it is part of my disposition as a leader. I breathe and eat this philosophy.

If I have a goal to grow my church by 10 people in the next 30 days but that is only a fad or program and isn't in my heart, that growth is not going to last because it is not part of my being. *The Kingdom Mind* must be instilled at the heart level and not in the head. I can't report exactly when this *Mind* became part of my makeup, but I can tell you it is there and there to stay. That is my ministry philosophy.

When I went to Bible college, I sat in a missions course taught by a woman who had been a missionary in Egypt. She was talking about Jesus when He gave the disciples the Great Commission in Matthew 28. Then she took us to Luke's account of the early church in Acts and pounded into our heads that missions was the work our churches and ministries were to be about. By the end of the class, it dawned on me that the Church should always be thinking about how it can impact a generation and how it can impact the city. That's where my heart for evangelism began.

Then I noticed that when we won people through evangelism, we didn't always do a good job of discipling them, so I determined that if and when I ever pastored a church, I would emphasize both outreach *and* discipleship training. I saw that people could learn how to come to church for two or three hours and behave quite properly. They would dress nicely and say all the right things. They would have church and leave satisfied with their church experience, but then go back on their stage and misbehave and not represent the Kingdom directives in His word.

Churches often had the numbers but the numbers did not necessarily contribute to carrying out the mission of the church. The Great Commission never goes out of style, and empowering people never goes out of style. Street and tent meetings may go out of style, but empowering people never goes out of style.

I began to talk about my development when I mentioned my missions class in Bible School. I want to go back even farther and share more of my journey describing how I came to lead in the first place and how I developed *The Kingdom Mind* I have today. This will help you better understand where I have come from so you can comprehend where God wants us to go. Join me as we go back there now.

KINGDOM MIND THOUGHTS

1. Jesus did not come preaching the Church; He came preaching the Kingdom.

2. The Great Commission has not been revoked and it is not out-of-date.

3. God is responsible for church growth, not the leaders.

4. Leaders must teach people to be good citizens of God's kingdom (discipleship), not good members of a church.

5. Leaders do their work first and foremost because they love God.

CHAPTER 3

MY LEADERSHIP JOURNEY BEGINS

As a young person, I was bashful and would not have been considered a people person. If anyone would have examined me, they would have concluded I was not the person most likely to succeed. I was a young man who felt most comfortable being around only certain people. My father was a preacher so I have always been a church kid, and of course we went to church every Sunday. My mother also took me to every prayer meeting. My parents made us be a part of every youth ministry church service that was being held. It was hard to step out and do anything if I was there by myself because I was so shy.

I maintained average grades but was active in school in Springfield, Ohio. I was involved but did not stand out and was an intramural athlete, but not on the high school football or basketball team. I played but wasn't good enough to make the team.

I thought I wanted to be an engineer, so of course I took algebra, trigonometry, and all the science courses. I felt good about myself because I had chosen engineering as my career. In my senior year of high school, however, my friend Peggy invited me to a church service. Since we were in a community choir, we had the opportunity to visit a variety of denominations because we got invited to many churches within the community.

Then on one occasion, Peggy invited me to come to her church for a choir rehearsal. I'd never been to this church because it was a Pentecostal church. I asked another friend to go with me because I didn't want to go by myself. I went to this one service, and I don't remember the title of the pastor's sermon, but he asked if anybody wanted to give his or her life to the Lord. Then the speaker started singing *I Surrender All*. At that point, I lost control and started crying. I was embarrassed because I was crying in front of both the girls with whom I had come. Yet before I knew it, I raised my hand, came forward, and was baptized that very day.

My dad said he did not want me going back to that church ever again, but my mom advised him to reconsider. I went back and received the baptism in the Holy Spirit about three months later. When I shared my experience with my parents, my father didn't feel too good about it, but my mother was quite excited. She called her aunt, our Aunt Mabel, to let her know and that's when I found out that my aunt went to a church in the denomination of the church where I had been baptized. My aunt was ecstatic because she had been praying for our entire family.

My aunt was a praying woman. If she was staying with us, I saw her praying when I went to school. If I came home from lunch at noon, she was praying. When I came back home from school, she was praying. When I went to bed at night, she was praying. She prayed consistently like that every day.

Aunt Mabel left a deep impression on my life. When anyone got sick, she would pray over handkerchiefs and send them in the mail to the sick. I had asthma when I was a child and my mother would put one of those hankies she sent over my chest. People wouldn't call my father the pastor when they needed prayer; they would call my Aunt Mabel.

IN THE MILITARY – ALMOST

After that, my first pastor, Elder Charles Scott taught me

how important it was to give attention to people. He was discipling and preparing me for a future I wasn't even aware of. I was seventeen years old and Elder Scott served as my mentor for about three years. During that time, I met my wife in a choir rehearsal. We had only been dating for three months when we started talking about getting married. I proposed to her when I was 19, but then I got a draft notice. I was to leave Springfield, Ohio and go to a place called Fort Hays where I was to receive my orders.

At some point during that same year, I had a minor asthma attack. I went to the doctor but he didn't have to do much for me. This doctor recommended that I take the records from my doctor that chronicled my history with asthma, just in case I had any problems in the army. Unfortunately, my family doctor had died and there were no records to access. The new doctor said the best he could do was to give me a letter based on my one visit, and he was not sure how useful or acceptable it would be with the military. This new doctor gave me a letter that stated,

To Whom It May Concern,
This person has experienced bouts with asthma.
Sincerely,
The Doctor

It was certainly short and sweet, but I took it. When my pastor read it, he said, "That sentence is not going to keep you from going to the army." The church had a farewell party for me, and I left Springfield on the bus to go to Fort Hays. When I got to Fort Hays, a lieutenant instructed anyone with a medical problem to form one line. A group of us complied and I noticed that all the guys with me had large envelopes, I assumed with their x-rays and medical files. The lieutenant passed them on through one-by-one and didn't deny anybody entrance into the military.

When he got to me he said, "Well?" I gave him the letter and he asked, "How do you feel?" I said, "I have shortness of breath." "That's all?" he responded. I said again, "Shortness of breath," and handed him the letter. He said "Okay, I'm going to permanently disqualify you." When he did that, I knew something was up, thinking, "Okay, Lord, why are you doing this? All the other men got in but You are sending me home." Little did I know that day would mark a turning point in my life.

"I'M GOING TO BE AN EVANGELIST."

After I got back, I moved to Columbus and got married. When we were first married, I spent a lot of time in prayer. After our first month of marriage, I Informed my wife that I was going to be youth president at the church and that I was also going to be an evangelist. I wanted to tell her so that when it happened, she would know I had really heard from the Lord.

A year later, I was president of the youth ministry, even though I had no experience or background in leadership. Never, ever had I done anything like that. I had an elected group of people who were with me in the ministry and we met every month to plan our meetings. Everything went well.

That's when my zeal for evangelism began. Back then, we conducted a street meeting on Monday night in various apartment complexes. I started something called the Apostolic Pentecostal Fellowship in the city, and shortly thereafter, I became the Southern District President in our organization. I then moved on from being the Southern District President to the Vice President of the State Young People and then to the State President of the Young People.

I also served as the coordinator of the state convention because Bishop Norman Wagner kept urging me to do different things that I was afraid or hesitant to do. He helped me discover that I could do some things that I thought I could not do. Events didn't stop there, and I moved on to become our national and then international president. It was during that time that I sensed the call to evangelistic ministry.

I still held those other leadership positions, but in 1975 I began my role as a full-time evangelist. My parents had seldom left Springfield but there I was getting on planes and going to places like London, Liberia in West Africa, and South America. My father thought I was crazy as I traveled to places I never thought I would see to do Kingdom work.

All of this happened and I never dreamed of or asked for it. I never asked for that stage or to be a coordinator or president. All I knew was that I gave myself fully in prayer to become the person God wanted me to be, and then those things started happening to me. I loved God and yielded myself to Him. That was and still is my ministry motivation. It should be yours too.

My wife was a tremendous support to me in those early years (and still is). I worked for a bank when I first got the call to full-time ministry. I was naïve enough to ask the bank if they could give me a leave of absence to pursue ministry. The manager said he could only do that if I went into the army, so I had to quit my job. Then we bought our first house, closing on the loan the day I quit my job. I only had one revival meeting planned for the following two months, and I told my wife that I could not watch her go to work while I was at home.

She said that we knew God had called me, and pointed out I wasn't going to be happy going back to work, and she was correct. I held that one meeting two months later, and then I booked another meeting in December and then another meeting in January. I started averaging one meeting a month but I didn't receive much money from those meetings. In fact, I couldn't count on much money at all. If I got anything, it was less than what I had earned at the bank.

All of a sudden, the door opened in 1976, and I stayed busy from that day forward. I marvel when I consider the outreach we did under the banner of the End Time Evangelistic Revival Crusade, which I founded. I started going to cities asking pastors if they would come together and sponsor the crusades, and they did. I went to Washington, D.C. every year and thought maybe we would settle there, but it was Columbus that would go on to figure prominently in our future as God's *Kingdom Mind* continued to take shape in our lives and ministry.

There were several individuals who were significant in my transition from the bank to full-time ministry. My first extended revival came through Bishop Richard Young. He invited me to Grand Rapids, Michigan where Elder Abney was the pastor. That was the door-opener for me and they encouraged me to consider going full-time in the ministry. I was hesitant at that time to consider this, but they played a key role in motivating and inspiring me to act on what was in my heart.

Bishop Ray E. Brown from Brooklyn, New York also encouraged me to go into ministry. In fact, I was attending an Elim [Aenon] Bible College celebration and he prophesied to me at that event. He didn't say anything I didn't know, but he certainly confirmed it. That was another experience that pushed me toward full-time ministry in terms of being an evangelist. Then a man named Marshall Taylor heard about me and told me he was going to tell his father-in-law, Pastor Hoodie Hoke, to encourage me by inviting me to Detroit to hold a revival in 1976. After I went to Detroit, my life changed and many more doors opened for me. From there, other exciting things happened that I will describe in the next chapter, including a transition to being a local church pastor.

KINGDOM MIND THOUGHTS

1. Leadership is a journey, not a destination.

2. Everyone has an assignment to fulfill for the Kingdom, and that assignment will take place on a specific, God-assigned stage, which in most cases is outside the church walls.

3. It is important for leaders to remember where they have come from so they can better relate to the journey that others are on.

4. Leaders should do what they do because they love God, not because they love the ministry.

CHAPTER 4
A CHURCH
IN COLUMBUS

The crusade we held in Columbus in the early days of my evangelistic ministry taught me a lot. It was around 1980, and we wanted to hold a crusade at a facility called the Veteran's Memorial, which seated about 3,000 people. Many people said it was impossible for an African American youth evangelist to rent a huge hall like the Vets, bring the churches together, and cover all the expenses as I was trying to do. My intention was to be a blessing to the city and its churches. Philip Locke, who was coordinator for that event and many others I led, believed we could do it and his faith was instrumental in us being successful.

I had studied Billy Graham and other groups, and my team felt confident that we knew how to pull off this Columbus crusade. The churches did indeed come together as we had planned. We rented the Vets Memorial, and, even though we didn't have any money, we paid for it. We saw many young people come to the Lord, and it was wonderful. I was reminded that when the Holy Spirit tells us to do something, it is always possible.

It was thrilling to see so many people giving their lives to the Lord everywhere we went. We would come to a city and see 100 to 150 young people surrender their lives to Christ. Then we started traveling with a choir. A woman named Sharon Johnson, who was a songwriter, traveled with our team. We developed a choir with the support of Thomas Adams to create an opportunity for her to share her music. It was exciting for us to sing the music she composed all around the nation.

When I got started in ministry, people created opportunities for me. Because they had done so, I wanted to create opportunities for other people to express their Kingdom gifts – I wanted to provide a stage for them. There were others along the way who I took with me and created opportunities for them as well. This is where my emphasis on empowering others came into focus. When I trained people in the way they should minister when people came forward, I saw firsthand the effectiveness of having trained people who were equipped with *The Kingdom Mind*.

Our altar workers asked those who were coming to give their lives to the Lord if they had ever been a member of the church or not. Did they want to receive the baptism in the Holy Spirit? Did they have special needs or need healing? The counselors knew what to do because I had trained them, and I am still training people today so they can be successful on their stage.

I did not travel to build or promote one specific church. Our crusades were an expression of God's kingdom and not conducted to establish one church. Obviously, we counseled those who came to the Lord that they needed to be in a church, but what we were doing was introducing people to God's kingdom as part of our Great Commission mandate.

By the time I got to be the international president as a youth leader, I had come a long way from a young man of 17 with no Pentecostal background or heritage. I had achieved my role without my father being a bishop and without having any special connections within my organization. From that position of youth leader president, the Lord transitioned me into pastoral work, and that was a major shift.

BECOMING A PASTOR

I had a sense that God wanted me to come off the road and serve as the pastor for a local church. I was praying about it, but I didn't want to pastor in Columbus. I made that quite clear to anyone who would listen – my wife, father, father-in-law, and church supervision. My father-in-law said, "You don't have a choice if the Lord says that is what He wants you to do," but I was still adamant about not doing it. Then while I was conducting a crusade in Birmingham, Alabama, I heard from the Lord while we were in prayer for the meetings.

During that prayer session, I had a clear vision in which the Holy Spirit said to me, "Here's a key. Take it and put it in the door." When I took the key and put it in the door, He said, "Turn and open it," and I obeyed. When I opened the door, a rush of water flooded the room where we were praying. Now that I look back, I realize I was having what some call a Pentecostal moment, and I immediately knew I was going to Columbus, because God had used the water to speak His will to me on one other occasion.

My first encounter with "water" was during a chapel service while I was still in Bible school. I was not thinking about being a pastor then; my focus was on conducting evangelistic crusades. The speaker that day was teaching from Ezekiel 47 and the vision Ezekiel had of the waters that started out ankle deep but ended in waters deep enough for swimming. In the vision, the water transformed everything in its path wherever it went.

During that message, I wrote down the notes and plans for how I was to going to conduct the crusades. I didn't know what to do with all the detailed notes I had, so I went to talk to Bishop Quander Wilson and showed him all that I written. He said, "Brother Tillman, don't ever lose those notes because I believe they describe what God is going to use you to do."

Therefore, when I saw the water rush into the room before the Birmingham crusade, I knew God was speaking to me again, this time about being a pastor as He had spoken to me about being an evangelist. I called my wife and said we're going to start the church and it will be in Columbus. I asked her not to tell her family, however, because I didn't want them to feel any pressure to be part of the church unless they felt led to do so.

We started the church in 1989 with nothing. I didn't have anything, having served as an evangelist since 1975 after giving my heart to the Lord in 1967. I didn't know how we were going to pay the rent on our meeting space. Each week, however, the money was there. Three years later, when it was apparent we were a viable and growing church, I knew we could not continue to rent space. We needed our own building.

OUR BUILDING

When we knew we needed our own building, there was a large piece of property across the street from where we lived at the time. Before we started the church, some people we knew came to our house and informed us that they were bidding on the property but they were quite early for the auction that day. They asked if they could wait in our house until it was auction time, which we allowed them to do.

Three years after we started the church, that property was still available. When I thought about it, I said to myself that we could not afford it, so why even pursue it? I could not get the thought of buying it out of my head, however, so I called the owners and set an appointment. My attorney came with me, and during the meeting, I informed the owners that we wanted to buy the property. I promised to give them $100,000 in cash, but would need time to pay off the balance.

They said they didn't normally do that but promised to get back to us. When they did, they agreed to my terms and we purchased the 45 acres (we have since purchased another two acres). In the meantime, a friend of mine called to and inform me that he had a trustee in his church who worked at Huntington Bank, and they were looking to do more business in the inner city.

We talked to the bank in December of 1992, and of course they wanted to look at our books, which were being done by an accounting firm at that time. They took the information back to the bank and the bank approved our loan. The vice president of the bank came to me at the King Center where we were renting space. I didn't have an office so had to meet with him in the kitchen, with pots and pans hanging from the ceiling. The vice president said they would give us a loan to build but only if the land was paid off, free and clear.

In March of 1993, we paid off the land from our weekly revenue of tithes and offerings. I had told the church we were not going to sell chicken and barbecue dinners to raise the money. I had taught the church that giving was a blessing, not selling. I used the example that it was appropriate to give our clothing away that we no longer used. We did not try and sell it to people who could barely afford it. I also did not want to hand out dime and quarter holders that some churches used to raise money for their building fund. I knew God did not want us going through the community begging for support to build a building in His name.

The tithes and the offerings are essential for the support of any church. We did not want to take advantage of people in the community to build God a house because they had nothing to do with the vision. I believed the people who were married to the ministry should be the ones who were to take full responsibility for our next step of construction and purchasing property to build a worship center. *The Kingdom Mind* required that our people give generously to build this house of worship.

I went back to the bank vice president and confirmed that the bank would finance a construction loan when we paid off the land. I showed him the deed, the bank kept their promise, and we started construction in September of 1993. We moved into the first building in June of 1994.

That's a summary of my life from 1967 until we moved into the church where we still are today. There is nothing more important or significant for any of us than when the Holy Spirit speaks to us. My life is based and has been built on that truth. I have learned not to put my trust in anyone but Him. The Lord uses people to open doors for us, but that only happens when we are trusting in Him.

KINGDOM MIND THOUGHTS

1. No matter how long leaders have served, they will never outgrow their need to operate in faith.

2. Faith is not an event; it is a lifestyle.

3. Leaders walking in their assignment on their stage are connected to all the resources they need to complete the task.

4. Leaders need to create opportunities for people to express their gifts and purpose, and to gain confidence that God is with them.

CHAPTER 5
INADEQUATE

Jesus discussed His role as shepherd in John 10:11-13:

"I am the good shepherd. The good shepherd lays down his life for the sheep. The hired hand is not the shepherd and does not own the sheep. So when he sees the wolf coming, he abandons the sheep and runs away. Then the wolf attacks the flock and scatters it. The man runs away because he is a hired hand and cares nothing for the sheep."

If we do what we do for any motivation besides our love for God, we are heading for trouble. We cannot be in ministry for money, prestige, benefits, or fame (yes, some of God's most anointed have garnered fame in secular society). If we are not careful, we can easily become professional clergy or leaders-for-hire, steeped in biblical principles and church growth theory but approaching our work as a job instead of a calling. The same can be true for those in secular positions not related to church work.

When we love God and surrender to His plan for our

lives, He then gives us a vision for what it is He wants us to do. He shows us the stage and assignment that belong to us, and that vision is what compels us to stay the course, even when persecution arises and things don't go well. It is love for God (and the vision) that causes leaders to face their inadequacy and receive God's assurance of help as they go forward. We will look more closely at loving the vision in the next section.

I shared with you a brief overview of my journey from when I met the Lord in 1967 to where I am today. Let's go back now and look at the call of Moses, and identify some parallels between what I learned and what Moses encountered as God called him to go back to Egypt and confront Pharaoh:

> The Lord said, "I have indeed seen the misery of my people in Egypt. I have heard them crying out because of their slave drivers, and I am concerned about their suffering. So I have come down to rescue them from the hand of the Egyptians and to bring them up out of that land into a good and spacious land, a land flowing with milk and honey—the home of the Canaanites, Hittites, Amorites, Perizzites, Hivites and Jebusites. And now the cry of the Israelites has reached me, and I have seen the way the Egyptians are oppressing them. So now, go. I am sending you to Pharaoh to bring my people the Israelites out of Egypt." But Moses said to God, "Who am I that I should go to Pharaoh and bring the Israelites out of Egypt?" And God said, "I will be with you. And this will be the sign to you that it is I who have sent you: When you have brought the people out of Egypt, you will worship God on this mountain. Moses said to God, "Suppose I go to the Israelites and say to them, 'The God of your fathers has sent me to you,' and they ask me, 'What is his name?' Then what shall I tell them?" God said to Moses, "I am who I am. This is what you are to say to the Israelites: 'I am has sent me to you.'" (Exodus 3:7-14).

Moses asked who he should say sent him when the people asked, and God instructed him to respond that "I am that I am" sent him. Moses still had more excuses why he could not go, so the Lord took their discussion a step farther:

> Moses said what if they will not believe me or listen to what I say? For they may say the Lord has not appeared to me. The Lord said to him, "What is that in your hand?" And he said, "A staff." And the Lord instructed him to throw it on the ground. He threw it on the ground and it became a serpent and Moses fled from it. The Lord directed Moses to stretch out his hand and grasp it by its tail. When he stretched out its tail and caught it, it became a staff in his hand. "This," said the LORD, "is so that they may believe that the LORD, the God of their fathers—the God of Abraham, the God of Isaac and the God of Jacob—has appeared to you."
>
> Then the Lord said, "Put your hand inside your cloak." So Moses put his hand into his cloak, and when he took it out, the skin was leprous—it had become as white as snow. "Now put it back into your cloak," he said. So Moses put his hand back into his cloak, and when he took it out, it was restored, like the rest of his flesh. Then the Lord said, "If they do not believe you or pay attention to the first sign, they may believe the second. But if they do not believe these two signs or listen to you, take some water from the Nile and pour it on the dry ground. The water you take from the river will become blood on the ground (Exodus 4:1-9).

God assured Moses that He would accompany him to Egypt, but Moses was not convinced. That's when the Lord gave Moses some startling signs of the power available to Moses when he went. First, God told Moses to throw down his shepherd's staff. If I had a staff, threw it down, and it became a snake, I would know there was something unusual going on! If God then said to take that serpent by the tail, I would be fearful that the snake could harm me.

When told to throw down his shepherd's rod, Moses was probably thinking, "That's only the rod I use as part of my vocation as a shepherd." God directed Moses to throw the rod on the ground because God was going to use it. God used the leprosy to show Moses His power to transform what seemed to be bad situations into normal ones.

People look for all kinds of lessons behind the rod and the leprosy. To me, they simply indicated to Moses that God could do whatever He said He was going to do. God was strengthening Moses' resolve regarding his assignment and teaching him to obey. God was also letting Moses know that He was with him to do whatever needed to be performed to carry out the divine objective God had given him. That's what we must know and believe in our hearts that God is with us and therefore we are going to lead effectively. If we don't believe that, we may as well go sit in the bleachers and watch the game. If we don't believe that, we can then look for techniques to ensure our success, and we seek to be professional clergy rather than obedient servants.

The Lord even told Moses that when he arrived in Egypt, he would be empowered to take water from the Nile, pour it on the ground, and watch it turn to blood. After all that, what was Moses' complaint? He said he was inadequate because he was slow to speak. After Moses had heard from the Lord, why would he bring up his slow speech? He did so to reiterate how inadequate he felt. God is with me to help me and to perform whatever needs to be done to fulfill the divine objective, but I can still look at what I don't have in the natural instead of what I have in the Lord.

WHEN INADEQUACY COMES

All leaders will have moments, maybe even seasons, in our leadership journey when we feel inadequate. That's not necessarily a bad thing because if we don't admit our inadequacy, we will try to fulfill our mission in the strength of our own egos. Then we are truly going to come up short because we don't have all the skills necessary to fulfill that divine objective – we will fail unless we acknowledge that we *don't* have what it takes. Moses' assignment would require that he speak and he lacked speaking skills. Moses could talk to his peers and his sheep, but God was sending him to talk to the most powerful man in the world. Moses didn't see how he could do that.

When I started out, one of my weaknesses I had not yet come to understand was the uniqueness of personalities. I've always been a perfectionist and because I was, I would make it difficult for everyone else because I thought everybody should be like me. I complained about people more times than I expressed appreciation. I didn't realize or recognize that those working with me should be appreciated, but I did not express that unless they did everything exactly as I wanted them to do. Most of these people were volunteers and very much wanted to be with me, work with me, and support me.

Therefore, when someone would address me about that weakness, I tended to take it personally and not search my heart and behavior to see if it was true. Instead, I would tell them but I didn't feel that way. I responded that I didn't know how they could think that was true. In my mind, just because I did not say thank you did not mean I did not appreciate what others were doing. After I matured, I then started to have more understanding of different personalities and their needs. I came out of my comfort zone and did something – express gratitude – that I did not normally do. I thanked people and told them they had done a good job.

There have been times when I didn't see how I was going to do what God wanted me to do as well. It was difficult for me to admit in my initial years of leadership that I lacked. I didn't want anyone to know that I lacked because I thought if I lacked, I wasn't good enough. Therefore, I tried to do everything. Then I found out I wasn't good at "everything," and I made a lot of mistakes because I was trying to be good at things I wasn't gifted or skilled to do.

When I was a youth worker, I was officiating a service for the youth, and my supervisor, Sister Dorothy Good, noted that I was frowning a lot. She came to me after the service and said that everyone knew what I was thinking and feeling by the expression on my face. She advised me that I did not want them to know what I was thinking in certain situations. She noticed that whenever something disturbed me, I frowned, and sometimes I frowned way too much and too often.

I protested and said I didn't do that but she held my feet to the fire and said, "Oh yes you do." Then someone else came along and told me the exact same thing. I got offended again because they said I frowned too much. After I thought about it for a while, I decided that maybe they were right and I had some things to learn about working with my team members.

Sometimes I have that tendency even now but not as much as I did then. Sister Good thought it would be good if I addressed that because she reminded me that I was an important person to everyone who was following my leadership. Everything I did and said meant something to the team, so I needed to ensure that if something went wrong, I should try *not* to show my displeasure but address it at a later time.

We leaders can become self-absorbed, self-conscious, and insecure when we are thinking about ourselves and what we should be doing or when we try to project the image of a strong, in-control leader. When that happens, we do not consider the other human assets who are around us. When we face our limitations, it frees God to provide what we need to ensure that the job gets done. That's why Paul wrote, "For we walk by faith, not by sight" (2 Corinthians 5:7).

THE INTENSITY OF THE CALL

God was not waiting for Moses to come to Him. God initiated contact with Moses and had an urgent message and responsibility for him to carry out. I can identify with the intensity with which someone's calling can come. We must get to the place when God talks to us that we grasp why He is coming at us with great intensity. We should not try to soften or diminish those encounters.

Why did He come at Moses with such intensity and clarity? He did so because He heard the cry of His people. God puts us in positons to do something for the same reason, because God heard the cry of His people in need. It wasn't about Moses, and it's not about you and me. It's about His people, most of whom we aren't even aware exist yet. It's about those lost souls we don't even know. It's about people dying in this world without God. That perspective must be part of *The Kingdom Mind* thinking.

When I first started leading, I knew I was not a detail person. I like big-picture thinking and usually let someone else fill in the blanks. I am not patient or energetic enough to handle the details. Therefore, I have to have people around me who fill in the blanks. I had to admit that I didn't like filling in the blanks and not be ashamed of it. I assumed that God had someone close to me who liked filling in the blanks. Since God has someone to fill in the blanks, why should I stress myself out trying to prove I'm a great leader with a skill set I don't have?

Great leaders are people who aren't ashamed to admit what they don't know. They don't care what anyone thinks about the fact that they don't know. They're going to get something done because they realize they need other human assets with skills they don't have to assist in accomplishing the divine objective God has given them.

Moses' encounter with the Lord almost didn't end well. Let's read from the Bible to learn what happened:

> But Moses said, "Pardon your servant, Lord. Please send someone else." Then the Lord's anger burned against Moses and he said, "What about your brother, Aaron the Levite? I know he can speak well. He is already on his way to meet you, and he will be glad to see you. You shall speak to him and put words in his mouth; I will help both of you speak and will teach you what to do. He will speak to the people for you, and it will be as if he were your mouth and as

if you were God to him. But take this staff in your hand so you can perform the signs with it" (Exodus 4:13-17).

Why was God angry? God performed many signs to show that He was adequate even if Moses was not, but Moses *still* doubted. It's then that God performed another sign for Moses: He identified Moses' ministry partner, his brother Aaron. God promised Moses that He would empower Aaron to speak on Moses' behalf to the people. Let's look more closely in the next chapter at this concept of ministry partners, who they are, and how important they are to ministry and leadership success.

KINGDOM MIND THOUGHTS

1. Leaders must face their inadequacies to do what God has assigned them to do.

2. God gives leaders urgent assignments because He hears the cries of people in need.

3. God will perform all the miracles needed for His leaders to carry out His assignments.

4. Leaders must admit that they don't know what they don't know and find others who do know what they don't.

CHAPTER 6
PARTNERS IN MINISTRY

Let's take a moment to review what we have discussed so far. This section is titled "Loving God," which may seem quite elementary. Deuteronomy 6:4-5 states, "Hear, O Israel: The Lord our God, the Lord is one. Love the Lord your God with all your heart and with all your soul and with all your strength." All ministry must emanate from our love for God and that is true for leaders as well as followers.

Matthew 20:26 then adds an important piece to our understanding of leadership: "Not so with you [who want to be leaders]. Instead, whoever wants to become great among you must be your servant." Let's examine this concept of service and leadership, which seems to be a contradiction of terms to some.

LEADERSHIP AND SERVICE

I have found that all people lead at some time in their lives. I referred to it earlier as our assignment or stage. If we are not employed by the church, we are employed elsewhere and lead companies, departments, or work teams. When we are not functioning as an employer or employee, we are operating in a leadership role as a neighbor, parent, volunteer, or student.

My point is that when we lead, whether it is the PTA, the garden club, or our child's football booster club, we should seek to be an influence in everything we do. Our love for God as His child should be the main stimulus behind every role or assignment, and loving God requires that we have the mindset of a servant. Charles Wesley penned the words, "To serve the present age, my calling to fulfill. Oh, may it all my powers engage to do my Master's will!" We are to be servants if we are leaders, which is where the term *servant leader* originated.

Jesus was a servant. He did not come to do His will but the will of Him who sent Him. He did not come to be served, He came to serve. Those who followed Jesus like Paul or Peter often proclaimed themselves to be a *doulos*, which is the Greek word for slave, and it stands for people who submit their will to the will of another. Disciples who follow Jesus always see themselves first as servants. To love God, we must love Him from the perspective of a servant of others, but of Him first and foremost.

When we serve God, we further realize that God is our source. If He is the source, then everything originates from Him – the assignment or stage, the direction, the skills, and the resources. Paul wrote, "I can do all things through Christ who strengthens me" (Philippians 4:13). When the Bible speaks of source, I think of Abraham who said that God was his *Jehovah-Jireh*, which translated means *the Lord will provide*. David stated, "The Lord is my shepherd, I shall not want (Psalm 23:1). Those men believed that their God provided their means. They didn't have a need that God could not meet. David realized he didn't have to experience want because the Lord was his source. If we understand the role of God as our shepherd, we know that He is responsible to lead and guide the sheep to a place where we have all we need to exist.

There is not anyone in the Bible for whom God did not take full responsibility for leading and guiding their lives. Since God is our source, we must understand as a leader following His direction that we are going to encounter an obstacle labeled *inadequacy* that will try to sidetrack or prevent us from completing our assignments. We will determine that we don't have enough money, or that we are not intelligent or gifted enough. That's why our love for God must be our top priority. What we encounter in life may appear to be contrary to that fact, but we can't fall into the trap of allowing the obstacle to bring us to a mindset of inadequacy.

BACK TO MOSES

Let's return to our study of Moses, who received an assignment from God to go and have a conversation with Pharaoh, the most powerful man in the world. He did not feel adequate to accomplish his assignment on his stage, even though God had directly spoken to him about what it was. Moses didn't think he had anything of value that would empower him to accomplish this task: "Please, Lord, I have never been eloquent. I know you need me to go, but I've never been good at speech" (Exodus 4:10).

Keep in mind he was not reading the Bible or hearing a still, small inner voice. He was speaking with God directly! The assignments God gives us are usually intimidating and beyond our capability to finish. That's why our love for God must be uppermost in our thinking and our main motivation. If Moses loved God in that situation, he had to believe God.

When Moses informed God that he was slow of speech, he gave God insight into himself that God already had; he wasn't giving God any new information. That's the other part about loving God. He is not only our source, but He knows everything about us. Therefore, when God gives us an assignment, He knows about our inadequacies from our perspective. When Moses raised his speech problem, God had a conversation with Moses, asking him who made his mouth, further asking who makes a man mute, deaf, or blind? (see Exodus 4:11). God attempted to inspire confidence in Moses that God was more powerful than Moses' limitations. He was promising to empower Moses' slow tongue and teach him what to say.

As Moses continued to protest, God gave another man

named Aaron an assignment. He directed him to go with Moses to Egypt and serve as his mouthpiece. Loving God involves learning how to trust God for the resources we need to fulfill our assignments – and that includes both human and supernatural resources. As a leader, I must understand that it's not a sign of weakness or a strike against my call to leadership when I request someone's help. God gave Aaron to Moses to be his mouthpiece.

Leaders must play the same role for their people that God played for Moses – positioning them to succeed. Sometimes I have to say to a member of my team, "You're not the best spokesperson for this. You're good behind the scenes or coming up the ideas, but you're not the one that we're going to use in public." It doesn't mean they are inadequate to serve God or to be part of the team. It doesn't mean they are not valuable. It simply means they have limitations. The same is true for me. If I can't do something, it doesn't diminish my leadership call or capability.

What did Moses experience in his meeting with God? Moses met God at the burning bush that burned but was not consumed. God spoke to him in such a way that Moses recognized and honored the voice of God. Moses obviously knew something from past experiences about God. The good news is that because he loved God, he didn't overlook Aaron, the human asset God had given him. He saw Aaron because God revealed him to Moses. God must open our eyes to see the value and purpose of those around us.

God then made an astonishing statement that Moses was going to be like God to Pharaoh, revealing God's purpose through Aaron, the mouthpiece. That is an excellent picture of the concept of one's stage that I referred to earlier. We will be like God to the people who encounter us on our stage. I am not insinuating that Moses would be *a god*; God said he would represent God and as far as Pharaoh was concerned, it would be just like an encounter with God when Pharaoh met with Moses and Aaron.

Let's summarize. God spoke to Moses. Moses accepted the responsibility, but listed his deficiencies in the light of this new responsibility. Moses faced the fact that God was the source of his adequacy, and that source was going to provide human help for the assignment. All this was because Moses loved God, and we must love God so we accept all the assignments He gives us – and the people He provides to help us fulfill the assignments.

Moses had to see his role, Aaron had to see his role, and neither one of them could be jealous of the other because of the different roles they had. The roles they had were playing a part in the fulfillment of the big goal that God had established for them, which was to go to Pharaoh and tell him to let the people go. Therefore, Moses and Aaron had to be open to the voice of the Lord. When they did, they had *The Kingdom Mind.*

OBEYING GOD

The voice of the Lord to Moses created an opportunity and need for the grace of God. The grace of God came to meet that need when the Lord directed Aaron to go and meet Moses in the wilderness. He met Moses at the mountain and kissed him, and then Moses told Aaron all the words the Lord had spoken to him. God first spoke to Moses to direct and prepare him, and then spoke to Aaron to assign him. It all flowed together beautifully, and God's model hasn't changed.

When we hear the voice of the Lord, it opens the door for the partnership, and there were two partnerships in Moses' story. There was the partnership with God, or what I call a vertical partnership, and the partnership with Moses and Aaron, which was a horizontal partnership. The partnership I have with God is by God's design and grace; it's God's plan and not my plan. If God is ordering the partnership, the leader can then reveal God's vision. This requires another expression of *The Kingdom Mind.* When we love God, we love others so that we can all remain in harmony to fulfill the one mission given to the leader. That is another expression of God's grace: our ability to work in teams!

There is another reason why we need to love God when we obey and accept our assignment. It is because people will disappoint us, betray us, fail us, abandon us, and try to alter or even kidnap the vision and mission. When they try to do those things, as Judas did to Jesus, we cannot abandon the assignment because we love God, and that love causes us to identify more people to replace the ones who have left for whatever reason. More on that later.

The leader, in this case Moses, and the appointee, in this case Aaron, had to speak with the same voice. An assignment cannot have two different voices. Moses' voice could not be different than God's, and therefore Aaron's voice could not be different than Moses' voice. They all had to be on the same page. When they assembled to talk to the people in the fourth chapter of Exodus, Aaron spoke all the words the Lord had spoken to Moses. He then performed the signs in the sight of the people. The leader spoke to the other leaders. The voices of influence then become dominant and the leader permitted Aaron to fulfill his assignment. The assignment he fulfilled was to talk and share with the people what the Lord had shared with them.

God was carrying the weight of Israel's deliverance on his shoulders as Moses obeyed him. Moses was not carrying the weight of the people, but rather carrying the weight of obedience. Moses had to confront the fact that the Egyptians were not going to let the people go. Every time something happened and God reinforced His involvement through signs and wonders, the Egyptians would intensify the pressure on the people. The deliverance of the people was still not on Moses' shoulders; it was on God's shoulders. All Moses was doing was being obedient.

When a leader loves and obeys God, the responsibility for the outcome is on God. He's the One who must make it happen. All God expects us to do is be obedient. The Bible says in Hebrews 11:6, "He that cometh to God must believe that he is and that he is a rewarder of them that diligently seek him" (KJV). God is always proactive; He initiates contact and communion with his leaders as was also the case with Elijah, Moses, David, and Samuel. In every instance, God came and gave them their assignments. The key to the fulfillment of the assignment was through each man's obedience that was borne out of his love for God.

Jesus later said if we love Him, we are to keep His

commandments. If we love Him, we should surrender to Him. If we love Him, we must be willing to make sacrifices for His will to be done in our lives: "Love me with all your soul, with all your heart, with all your mind, and with all your strength," as God said in Deuteronomy 6:4-5.

Our love for God stems from His proactivity. If we look in Romans 5:8, we are told God was loving us while we were yet sinners. While I was yet a sinner, Christ loved me; He was coming for me before I ever knew anything about Him. He was serving me before I came to an understanding of His death for me. His coming to me was the reason why I fell in love with Him. My falling in love with Him put me in a place where I can live in obedience to Him, which we will look at in the next chapter.

KINGDOM MIND THOUGHTS

1. The leadership life is a life of service, no matter where a leader's stage is.

2. We need two partnerships if we are to be successful on our assigned stage. The first is our vertical relationship with God; the second is our horizontal relationship with our ministry or leadership partners.

3. We love God because He first loved us.

4. Love for God must be our ministry motivation because people will disappoint and fail us, even when we do everything correctly.

CHAPTER 7
OBEDIENCE

Let's look again at Jesus' words in the Lord's Prayer; "Your will be done on earth as it is in heaven." For His will to be done on earth, His Kingdom subjects with *The Kingdom Mind* must discover and do His will in a way that is pleasing to Him. The ends do not justify the means in God's kingdom. We cannot ignore His will, but when we find it, we cannot carry it out in any way that seems appropriate to us because we are leaders. *We must do God's will God's way.*

Obedience is an important indicator that I love God. If I'm not obeying Him, I tell Him that He is not a priority in my life and I don't value Him as much as I value something or someone else. My love for God must be more than theory, talk, or mental assent. It must be behavioral agreement – I align my behavior with His requirements. It goes beyond, "I hear God talk to me and I'm afraid. I heard God talk to me but I don't know if I can." It must become, "I hear God and I'm going to implement His will with His help."

Our behavior manifests our faith. If we are not pursuing

His will, then we are telling God that we don't believe Him and we can't carry it out. Believing in God and doing something for God are two different things. Let that statement sink in for a moment: *Believing in God and doing something for God are two separate practices.* We can believe and love God, but still be intimidated by what God wants us to do. Intimidation is the result of our own fear and flawed perception of what we see and who we are in Him.

I call it a pre-analysis of a not-yet-given response and outcome. We figure in our mind that if we do this or that, then this or that may be the outcome. If I was in Moses' place, I would have assumed that the people were not going to respond to me, or that Pharaoh was going to make my life difficult. The pre-analysis of the not-yet-given response can cause us to live in fear before we pursue God's will, just like it did Moses.

We must think that if God wants us to do it, then God will assist us in the implementation. Our eyes and analysis of the situation can fail us. The circumstances can seem bigger than God, and then we can worship at the feet of our fear, pain, and the outcome that has not yet taken place because we believe it's inevitable. Then we make that end our focus and deny God the right to control our lives because of what we see (or think we see in our limited perspective).

We cannot allow our eyes to lead us to failure. We must allow what God said to us to be the dominant picture over what we see, hear, or feel. Our feelings can get in a way of our love for God. When the people resist our leadership or when problems arise, we must allow our love for God to overcome and overwhelm those things so we can act.

We don't learn patience unless we are put in a position where we must be patient. It's the same with leadership, for we don't learn a different style or approach to leadership until we encounter different, challenging scenarios. We don't learn how to work with unique personalities or learn people's God-given skill sets until we are put together to work with those people. We learn to use a diverse group of people because they have a skill set that will help us achieve a specific goal.

We need everybody on our teams to learn how to appreciate their skill set and not think that they are being diminished or devalued because we are using someone else before we use them. If we love God and lead people, we love people. When we love people, they become so important that we will tell them we care about them. We can't be afraid to tell people that we love them. Loving them means that we are going to function with their best interests in mind. What is their best interest? If we are leaders, it is using them to achieve the ultimate goal we are trying to accomplish. When we implement that, it is in part because we are looking out for them and providing a stage.

PERSONAL IMPLICATIONS

If I love God, I'm not going to abuse or take advantage of the people with whom I am working. I am going to love them the way He loves me. I realize that He loves me despite all my issues and failures. I then stay focused on my relationship with God so I can have the right relationship with others. I am required to be honest about my relationship with God that helps me to be more forgiving so I can unconditionally love and be patient with them. It helps me to work with them as they grow because I understand my relationship with Him, and understand how patient He has been with me.

I know that I haven't always been what I needed to be and done what I should have done. If I can remember that and keep it as part of my *Kingdom Mind*, then it improves my relationship with other people. I try to interact with people in the ways and with the lessons with which God has interacted with me. I must always look in the mirror and see myself. God didn't quit on me when I did something I should not have done, or neglected to do something I should have. He stayed right there with me. I must do the same with people who are called to me, who are the human resources for accomplishing my assignment.

When I love God, I will be able to give people that same love. When they receive that love, they begin to trust me. Not all will, but for those who do trust me it means that they will follow my leadership because they have confidence that I have heard and am hearing from the Lord. I facilitate our trust relationship when I show and they see my love for them and for God. If they don't see my love for God, then it's going to be difficult for them to follow me because I am supposed to represent God to them, as Moses did to Pharaoh.

The key to my leadership success is that my love is predicated on what Jesus Christ did for me. What Jesus did for me doesn't mean too much if I don't remember the trauma in my life before He came into it. Before I came to the Lord, my life was in total dysfunction with a large chasm between the Creator and me. I was facing eternal damnation, but Jesus came to save me from the eternal death. Jesus solved my root problem, which is sin, and took the sting out of death.

When I think of my condition before Jesus, I think of the example Jesus provided in Luke 16:19-31:

> "There was a rich man who was dressed in purple and fine linen and lived in luxury every day. At his gate was laid a beggar named Lazarus, covered with sores and longing to eat what fell from the rich man's table. Even the dogs came and licked his sores. "The time came when the beggar died and the angels carried him to Abraham's side. The rich man also died and was buried. In Hades, where he was in torment, he looked up and saw Abraham far away, with Lazarus by his side. So he called to him, 'Father Abraham, have pity on me and send Lazarus to dip the tip of his finger in water and cool my tongue, because I am in agony in this fire.'
>
> "But Abraham replied, 'Son, remember that in your lifetime you received your good things, while Lazarus received bad things, but now he is comforted here and you are in agony. And besides all this, between us and you a great chasm has been set in place, so that those who want to go from here to you

cannot, nor can anyone cross over from there to us.'
"He answered, 'Then I beg you, father, send Lazarus
to my family, for I have five brothers. Let him warn
them, so that they will not also come to this place of
torment.' "Abraham replied, 'They have Moses and
the Prophets; let them listen to them.' ""No, father
Abraham,' he said, 'but if someone from the dead
goes to them, they will repent.' "He said to him, 'If
they do not listen to Moses and the Prophets, they
will not be convinced even if someone rises from the
dead.'"

The rich man saw Lazarus in the bosom of the Father
while he was in this all-consuming pain. He was in the fire and
wanted someone to cool his tongue. Abraham responded that he
could not send Lazarus to him, explaining that eternal death is
like being in a place where someone wants to die, but can't die.
Being separated from God is like being in pain when the pain
won't go away.

It's like the person who came to church to testify that she
was in a car accident but her life was spared. The car hit her, then
turned her car around and totaled it, but she walked away from
the accident. My life situation was worse than that car accident
because I was eternally separated from God. My life was a car
wreck that I walked away from because of Jesus. That eternal sep-
aration from God was only resolved through Jesus Christ, and
that's why I love Him – and then love His people.

If I don't have that kind of love, I will fill it with something
else. I will love my role as a leader more than I love God. If I love
leadership more than I love God, I won't act with *The Kingdom
Mind* because I will do whatever I must do to maintain my leadership. If things get rough, I may quit, and I'll use the people or
lack of resources as an excuse. I may stop serving the people and
insist that they serve me.

I'll find all kinds of excuses for my poor leadership because I love my role as a leader and love being over the people
more than God. When I love God and the people don't respond,

what am I going to do? If I love God, their coming or going will never stop me because I love Him. His love trumps any disobedience, lack of resources, and all the inadequacies I may personally have. The love He has for me is love that sustains me to accept and finish the assignment. It's the love for Him and what Jesus did for me that sustain me when I'm having trouble as a leader.

FAITH

I always refer to faith texts when I am training someone for leadership or looking for a weakness in my own role as a leader. For instance, if we have faith as a grain of mustard seed, we can say to the mountain, be thou removed, and the mountain will move and nothing will be impossible to us (see Matthew 17:20). Our tendency is to look for the mountain or obstacle that is outside of us, when really, the mountain is usually on the inside of us.

The mountain will only be conquered when I have the will to conquer it. Climbing the mountain may seem far beyond my ability, but the fear of climbing the mountain is the problem, not the mountain itself. If I have faith as a grain of mustard seed, then I can say to the mountain inside of me, "Be thou removed," and the mountain will be moved.

Two other faith verses that are relevant are found in Romans 10:17: "Now faith cometh by hearing and hearing by the word of God," and "We walk by faith and not by sight (2 Corinthians 5:7). Faith is stimulated by what we hear. For example, Abraham and Moses were both stimulated to action by what God said to them. Paul was also moved by what God said to him. The stimulus always comes from what God says.

Our faith is a response to what God says. Faith doesn't happen on our own, for God participates in our process of believing. Faith is never allowing the inward challenge or the outward situation to interfere with our walk with him. Faith is taking God at His word and then implementing that word.

Leaders need to have experiences that assist them in the development of their faith. When I spoke to my wife that I was going to be a leader even though I hadn't been a leader up to that point in my life, I had been thinking about what I told her for more than a year. I felt an inward push that went beyond what I thought I could do. My mind was having a hard time conceiving it, but I was being pushed from within. That's what happens whenever grace is operating. I needed to replace my mind with *The Kingdom Mind*.

Grace operates through an internal spiritual surge that we can't explain. Oftentimes, our mind is not on the same page as the push. In our mind, there's fear and apprehension. There's a push inside of us that we're going for something, despite all kinds of analysis (and negative feedback) about what it is God wants us to do. It's an inward push we can't explain. When people talk to us about it, we say we don't know except that we are being pushed to do it. We don't have the money, but we feel that we are supposed to do this. Then our faith grows when we obey the push; then we experience the outcomes that occur because we have obeyed.

When the Holy Spirit pushes you towards the assignment that God is giving you or the stage God has put before you, you will make an impact in someone else's life. That impact or influence is so rewarding that when the push comes again, and it always does, you are less reticent to obey. You recognize the prompting and you are not guessing about its source any longer. You used to guess, but you now know the push indicates something you need to do. That is also labeled maturity.

I was on vacation not too long ago and I took with me the book *Simple Church*. I read that book and it flipped my switch because before I read it, the Spirit had been talking to me about how to make a large church seem like a small church. That is exactly what *Simple Church* was all about. The book gave me the necessary push to come back home and tell all my leaders to read the book, informing them that we were going to make a shift to the *Simple Church* format.

As a leader, it's about hearing the voice of God first and then acting on what He said. I trusted I had heard the voice because I had some prior experience. It all started when I told my wife I was going to be youth president within the year. I had heard the Lord speak and put my trust in that. It happened and has been happening like that ever since. When we went into full-time ministry, we purposely didn't tell my wife's parents what we were doing because we didn't know how they were going to respond. They could have been upset, wondering why I was quitting my job, but I knew this was what God wanted me to do. If we were broke, then let us be broke. If we didn't have enough money, then we wouldn't have enough money. God, however, never let us down.

I came home one day and we had no food in the refrigerator and no money to buy any. My mother-in-law, who was unaware of our situation, called to say that she had some food in the house and was bringing it over. It's been like that for more than 40 years. God has always provided. I am an apprehensive traveler on airplanes, but in terms of doing what God wants me to do, I'm not apprehensive. I know He's in charge when I carry out His will, because I know He loves me. There is somebody else He's trying to reach and we must understand that somebody else's life is going to be impacted by this push that God is initiating. Lives, communities, and even countries are at stake when God's grace creates a push in our lives.

Our prayer communication with God helps us in the process of loving him. That communication with Him is one of the other keys points that is overlooked when we discuss building a successful ministry – or life for that matter. Prayer builds a relationship that enables us to find our stage and carry out our assignments. Prayer is the means through which we form *The Kingdom Mind*. It's not only reading His word or focusing on the fact that He died for us. It's also focusing on the fact that ongoing communication with Him is crucial because our assignments emanate out of prayer. When we hear God speak in prayer, we are not hearing it from a third party or through the mouth of preacher. We are hearing God with our own ears and heart. More on prayer later in Section Four.

I hope it is clear by now that your foundation for both *The Kingdom Mind* and your Kingdom stage is loving God. His love is what starts you out, directs you, sustains you, provides for you, and then starts the process all over again as your stage expands or changes. In the next section, we will examine the concept that once your love for God is activated and you have a stage, then you must find and love the vision that God has for you on that stage, where there will be multiple actors as we have already pointed out (we never accomplish the vision alone). Let's move on to the section on vision now.

KINGDOM MIND THOUGHTS

1. Obedience is the proof that you love God.

2. You must remember how God has loved you so you can love others in the same manner.

3. Maturity is recognizing the Holy Spirit's push that has come in the past.

4. *The Kingdom Mind* requires faith to act on what God said to do.

SECTION TWO
LOVE THE VISION

CHAPTER 8
LOVE THE VISION?

I am keeping each of the four sections in this book consistent by starting the title with the word *love*. This is the only section that I considered making an adjustment and using the word *accept*. When we love the vision, we accept what God reveals and then we pursue what He has revealed. When we pursue it, we then see it as God does, and we know His revealed will for our lives, which is our assignment on our stage.

You notice that the title of this chapter has a question mark and is not a straightforward statement. It may seem to follow that if someone loves God, then they will automatically love or accept the vision that God gives them for the stage prepared for them. I have found that this isn't necessarily the case, for the sense of inadequacy or the distaste for the vision may be strong enough to cause someone to avoid and even resent the vision.

An example of someone who loved God but did not love or accept the vision was the prophet Jonah. Jonah must have loved God, for he was considered a prophet before God ever sent him on his mission to Nineveh. He knew the Lord and God's great love for people, so I would assume Jonah knew God's love for him. Let's look at this story, which may be one of the best-known stories in the Bible:

> The word of the Lord came to Jonah son of Amittai: "Go to the great city of Nineveh and preach against it, because its wickedness has come up before me." But Jonah ran away from the Lord and headed for Tarshish. He went down to Joppa, where he found a ship bound for that port. After paying the fare, he went aboard and sailed for Tarshish to flee from the Lord (Jonah 1:1-3)

Most people assume Jonah ran because he hated the Ninevites. That may be true, but perhaps he was trying to save his own nation, for the Ninevites were cruel and Israel's enemies. If they repented and were spared, in Jonah's mind, it was tantamount to preserving them to attack Israel one day. Whatever his motivation, Jonah tried to flee the vision God had shown him.

When a storm arose that would not subside, the sailors found out that Jonah was running from God and at Jonah's request, they threw him overboard. After that act, the storm calmed down and the sailors marveled. That wasn't the end of the story, however: "Now the Lord provided a huge fish to swallow Jonah, and Jonah was in the belly of the fish three days and three nights" (Jonah 1:17). While in the fish, Jonah prayed a beautiful prayer, surrendering himself anew to God's will. Once again, it is clear that he loved God. After three days, the fish spit Jonah up onto a beach and he went to Nineveh to declare the word of the Lord:

> "Forty more days and Nineveh will be overthrown." The Ninevites believed God. A fast was proclaimed, and all of them, from the greatest to the least, put on sackcloth. When Jonah's warning reached the king of Nineveh, he rose from his throne, took off his royal robes, covered himself with sackcloth and sat down in the dust. This is the proclamation he issued in Nineveh:

"By the decree of the king and his nobles: Do not let people or animals, herds or flocks, taste anything; do not let them eat or drink. But let people and animals be covered with sackcloth. Let everyone call urgently on God. Let them give up their evil ways and their violence. Who knows? God may yet relent and with compassion turn from his fierce anger so that we will not perish." When God saw what they did and how they turned from their evil ways, he relented and did not bring on them the destruction he had threatened (Jonah 3:4b-10)

Because the people in Nineveh repented, God relented of His judgment, but Jonah was still holding out hope that God would follow through and destroy the city. When God did not, Jonah was angry and uttered these words:

He prayed to the Lord, "Isn't this what I said, Lord, when I was still at home? That is what I tried to forestall by fleeing to Tarshish. I knew that you are a gracious and compassionate God, slow to anger and abounding in love, a God who relents from sending calamity. Now, Lord, take away my life, for it is better for me to die than to live." But the Lord replied, "Is it right for you to be angry?" (Jonah 4:2-4).

Jonah loved God but he did not love the vision. He was angry and expended a lot of energy trying to avoid the vision and then fretting when the vision did not turn out as he had hoped it would. In this section, we want to look at what it will take for you to love the vision and how your love for the vision will show up in your life, the life you live on your stage, and the lives of the people who follow you.

VISION

The first aspect of vision is that it is the revealed will of God. Vision gives us direction, and the vision appears when God actually shares His thoughts with us. That revelation is a specific assignment or command from the mind of God to His body. When there is vision, it is always a joint venture, often accompanied by the words "let us." As we discussed in the previous section, many different gifts embodied in many different believers will be required to finish the task, as Paul taught us in Romans 12:4-8:

> For just as each of us has one body with many members, and these members do not all have the same function, so in Christ we, though many, form one body, and each member belongs to all the others. We have different gifts, according to the grace given to each of us. If your gift is prophesying, then prophesy in accordance with your faith; if it is serving, then serve; if it is teaching, then teach; if it is to encourage, then give encouragement; if it is giving, then give generously; if it is to lead, do it diligently; if it is to show mercy, do it cheerfully.

We all should operate based on the favor or grace that God has given us for those gifts. Where there is no vision, the people are careless and misdirected in their lives and don't utilize their gifts properly, if at all, as the writer of Proverbs warned: "Where there is no vision, the people perish" (Proverbs 29:18 KJV).

Vision defines why something exists, and everyone must know what their role is if the vision is to become a reality. Take for example, the tabernacle of God. God gave Israel and Moses a vision for the tabernacle. Joshua also had a vision passed down to him from Moses about the destiny of Israel when God said, "Moses my servant is dead; now therefore arise, go over this Jordan, thou, and all this people, unto the land which I do give to them, even to the children of Israel" (Joshua 1:2 KJV).

Jesus gave His disciples the vision in the New Testament when He said, "Go ye therefore, and teach all nations, baptizing them in the name of the Father, and of the Son, and of the Holy Ghost: Teaching them to observe all things whatsoever I have commanded you: and, lo, I am with you always, even unto the end of the world. Amen" (Matthew 28:19-20 KJV). Vision animates, inspires, and transforms purposeful vision into action steps.

Someone once said that vision occurs when people see what they aren't prepared to see. The people receive new thoughts and ideas, and *The Kingdom Mind* is shaped by and around those thoughts and ideas. We therefore are to live each day as a response to a vision that expands the message and influence of Jesus Christ. The vision cannot move forward without buy-in from many people. The concept of "let us" calls us to commit ourselves to what has been revealed. Personal buy-in is the acceptance of, agreement with, and commitment to a specific concept or course of action after which people contribute their effort and support. Therefore, we come together around the vision.

Buy-in is not offered as a response or favor to a leader, but it's a response to the grace of God. If we come together around anything but the vision, someone deemed that act as embezzlement. Using personal charisma, instead of godly vision, as a means to get things done is manipulation. The vision belongs to and centers around Jesus Christ and we must be careful not to steal His glory. He says, "I am the Lord: that is my name: and my glory will I not give to another, neither my praise to graven images" (Isaiah 42:8 KJV).

An example of buy-in is when Israel went home after Moses gave them the architectural blueprint for the tabernacle to decide how they would be involved. All the people who wanted to give to that project did so freely, not giving to Moses but rather to God. They brought so much that Moses had to turn them away and say enough: "Then Moses gave an order and they sent this word throughout the camp: "No man or woman is to make anything else as an offering for the sanctuary." And so the people were restrained from bringing more, because what they already had was more than enough to do all the work (Exodus 36:6-7).

That is the power of vision and the goal we want to achieve as leaders, regardless of wherever we function on our stage. Then God equipped and assembled skilled men together to be able to produce what He wanted:

Then Moses summoned Bezalel and Oholiab and

every skilled person to whom the LORD had given ability and who was willing to come and do the work. They received from Moses all the offerings the Israelites had brought to carry out the work of constructing the sanctuary. And the people continued to bring freewill offerings morning after morning. So all the skilled workers who were doing all the work on the sanctuary left what they were doing (Exodus 36:2-4).

We see that it was the grace of God providing both the resources and the structure for the vision. It was also the grace of God enabling men to structure the tabernacle precisely as He wanted it built with the gifts He had bestowed on them.

When the people gave, they made investments in the Kingdom with a *Kingdom Mind*. They did not have to be coerced or pressured. Israel released the resources required to move the vision forward because they were responding to the grace of God, which gave them a model of how God wanted them to worship Him not just then, but all the time. Making investments in the Kingdom should be the number one priority for our people and leaders. We cannot squander the wealth of our resources that God provided for the vision. Buy-in charges and changes nothing, but once there is buy-in, there is a cost in terms of time, money, and energy.

A let-us vision calls us to properly administer the resources provided to bring the vision to fruition, where God is then revealed. We must manage the human, financial, and grace-gift resources. Ephesians 3:2-3 states, "Surely you have heard about the administration of God's grace that was given to me for you, that is, the mystery made known to me by revelation, as I have already written briefly" and in Colossians 1:25: "I have become its servant by the commission God gave me to present to you the word of God in its fullness." Paul had a vision for the church but then had to organize or manage the vision and the resources to see it accomplished.

THE PROBLEM

A problem arises in Kingdom work when the vision is not let-us, but let-me and then you help me. When leaders make the vision theirs instead of God's, those leaders must employ all sorts of "techniques" to get the people on board and to keep them there. That is where our event-driven ministries have gotten into trouble. The way they got the people, which is events, is the way they must work to keep the people, which is more events. That is not *The Kingdom Mind*, but rather a business or entertainment mind. What's more, the vision will cost something when people and the leaders buy in. It is then that each person must do what Jesus said:

> "Whoever wants to be my disciple must deny themselves and take up their cross and follow me. For whoever wants to save their life will lose it, but whoever loses their life for me will find it. What good will it be for someone to gain the whole world, yet forfeit their soul? Or what can anyone give in exchange for their soul? For the Son of Man is going to come in his Father's glory with his angels, and then he will reward each person according to what they have done" (Matthew 16:24-27).

Once again, I refer to Jesus' prayer, "Thy kingdom come, *thy will be done* on earth as it is in heaven." *The Kingdom Mind* battles all other thoughts that do not help extend or build God's kingdom:

> Those who live according to the flesh have their minds set on what the flesh desires; but those who live in accordance with the Spirit have their minds set on what the Spirit desires. The mind governed by the flesh is death, but the mind governed by the Spirit is life and peace. The mind governed by the flesh is hostile to God; it does not submit to God's law, nor can it do so. Those who are in the realm of the flesh cannot please God (Romans 8:5-8).

We must put aside all our wishes and desires when we see the Kingdom to be a part of it. We must learn to live as a new creation, as Jesus said,

> Jesus answered, "Very truly I tell you, no one can enter the kingdom of God unless they are born of water and the Spirit. Flesh gives birth to flesh, but the Spirit gives birth to spirit. You should not be surprised at my saying, 'You must be born again'" (John 3:5-7).

Our cultures, both church and societal, sometimes work against establishing a Kingdom culture. We want to be like the world, we want to entertain or have a big choir. God wants to give us a vision and that vision will require all that we have and all that we are. God isn't interested in part-time residents of His kingdom, who give Him an hour or two a week. He wants them to serve full-time. That does not mean that everyone must be in full-time church ministry, but they must be full-time representatives of His kingdom in every role of life: work, family, neighborhood, and church.

In the next chapter, I want to discuss how important it is to empower the people in the pews if we are going to successfully fulfill our vision in our churches. If we love the vision, then we will love the work of building up the people so they can play a major role in seeing the Kingdom advance.

KINGDOM MIND THOUGHTS

1. Godly vision is a "let-us" vision; it requires multiple people to achieve.

2. Loving God does not guarantee that anyone will love His vision.

3. Leaders must not coerce or manipulate people to give or follow.

4. *The Kingdom Mind* requires a total commitment, which involves picking up a cross and following Jesus.

CHAPTER 9
THE PEOPLE IN THE PEWS

God gave me a vision for how to build an effective church in my early days as a youth leader. Even then, I noticed that many people coming to the church had received more than enough instruction and information, but there were some coming who didn't have enough. People were always at different points in their spiritual journey.

I had a vision that a church could connect the two groups – the haves and the have-nots – and I knew it would create quite an impact. If we could get those who had to impart what they had to those who didn't, and then those who received would in turn share what they learned with somebody else, we would have a discipleship chain or network that would cause the church to grow. That is what I have tried to do since 1975 when I began New Covenant Believer's Church.

CHURCH GROWTH

Church leaders must not forget the value and importance of empowering the people in the pews. If we can influence them with information and principles of the Kingdom, and develop in them *The Kingdom Mind* so they can use that information to impact others, then church growth will become automatic. Pastors and church leaders should not worry about growth because if they empower people, there will be growth. If leaders are thinking about the people who are not there, however, they will soon forget about the people who are present. Their focus will be on programs to get those who aren't there to come so they can fill the pews and supplement those who are already there.

The people who are present in the pews are the ones who are going to go and impact the world where they live. We must empower them and then the principle that Paul described as one sowing and another watering (see 1 Corinthians 3:7) will cause the growth. We won't have to worry about the harvest because that's not our responsibility anyway. It's God who gives the increase.

If God doesn't give the increase, too often we try and come up with marketing strategies to figure out how we can get the church to grow. I'm not saying there is necessarily anything wrong with that, but the bottom line is influencing people, not the numbers in the pews. Sheep produce sheep, and if that's true, then we should feed the sheep we have so those sheep will have sheep and then those sheep will produce more sheep, and we will have a growing church.

That's why it is so important to love the vision that God gives, not the vision that culture imparts. *The Kingdom Mind* will cause us to listen and do what God wants and do it the way God wants it done. Jesus did not talk about numbers in a church, but He did talk about discipling the nations. When we disciple people, the church will grow. When we love a vision of what we have seen someone else do or what we think church should be, then often we go off on tangents and don't keep the main thing the main thing.

DISCIPLESHIP

Discipleship starts with the information and principles of how God's kingdom functions so that people grasp who they are as citizens in that Kingdom. Our members are not only church-goers but also people for whom Jesus Christ died so they could enjoy a new life that is eternal. Their first allegiance is to Jesus and not their church or leadership. The life that He has given us has impacted us in such a way that it bears fruit and that fruit is valuable on our stage, which is our sphere of influence as well as where we go to church.

I'm passionate about discipleship in my remaining years of ministry. That's why we need *The Kingdom Mind* so we know that people are given to us to empower them and not to fleece or take advantage of them. We are not to use them to feed our event-driven programs. We are not to hold them through the power of our personal charisma or our charismatic spiritual gifts. We as leaders are to use the power of the Word in the love of God to help them in every area of their lives so they can experience the full impact and blessing of that and be a blessing to someone else on their stage. While that benefits the people, it is also an important part of loving the vision, for without the people, there will be no fulfillment of the vision.

I'm concerned for the part of the body of Christ of which I am aware and in which I work because many things we do are event-driven. I have no specific person or leader in mind, but I hear of and see masses of people coming together. Then we use charismatic gifts like prophecy or dynamic music that allows a gifted person to hold the attention of the people in the audience. The people become emotional and they don't think about what's happening or why it's happening to them. They override or disable their discernment, and they stop making it about God's kingdom and make it about what they can receive or how they feel. They can't be transformed because transformation comes from a re-newed mind (see Romans 12:1-2), and they have stopped think-ing to experience something that comes and goes – and when it goes, then they go someplace else looking for another experience.

We get caught up in the moment, looking for the spectac-ular instead of focusing on and taking advantage of the fact that Jesus Christ already did something spectacular. Even though we weren't there and didn't see it with our eyes, we can be blessed because we believe even though we did not see, as Jesus said to Thomas in John 20:29: "Because you have seen me, you have believed; blessed are those who have not seen and yet have believed." The blessing isn't in the spectacular event; it's faith in Christ and newness of life.

Faith must carry over into every area of people's lives. When we apply the principles of faith to marriage, to being a parent, or to the workplace, we will see spectacular transformation in our followers. We are not to allow them to enjoy watching someone else on their stage; each person is to have his or her own stage and act out their faith on that stage. We need to teach people to accept and thrive on the stage they are given. I know that I'm on my stage, and I'm going to represent the Kingdom to the best of my ability with everything in me. All that is important because the Church must think of itself as a therapeutic community that helps people understand and apply the principles of the Kingdom.

In the 1990s, I said to my wife and church leaders that mental health was going to become a relevant, important issue that the church needed to address. I said that we could not ignore it and therefore directed our people to get ready to address that issue. That's not an event-driven initiative or program. In response to that, we sent many of our people to special seminars over a two- or three-year period so they could be prepared to meet this need head-on as counselors when it became evident.

The goal was not to make everyone a counselor, but to train those in the pews to help others sitting in those pews with mental health challenges. That led us to establish marriage counseling as well as a significant premarital counseling program. Today, our church has a vibrant, effective counseling ministry and, sure enough, the people with mental problems, or those who were finally ready to admit their problems, can come and get the help they need.

I did not address what I sensed concerning mental health by having a conference that brought in speakers and prophets to speak to the mental health issues in one weekend. We equipped people over time to meet the coming need. We understood that we were and are to be a holistic ministry to help and empower people in every area of life, not just church life. We must do this with the tools and gifts God has given us. That is discipleship and part of loving the vision.

A WORD TO PASTORS

If you are a pastor, please hear what I am saying. I am *not* saying that church services and meetings are not important. They are, but the church is not primarily programs or a building; the church is people. People not only have needs, they have a purpose, gifts, and a calling to represent Christ, and they must be taught how to fulfill that purpose and use those gifts in the sphere where God has called them to serve, which I am calling their stage. Sometimes we forget that the people in the church go to more places than we leaders can go, for our lives are spent in church, but most of their lives are spent outside the church.

Years ago when I was a youth leader, we would have a street meeting or an outreach in a certain location. Maybe we would go there once a month and say that we were evangelizing. Sometimes 100 people would go with me, but it was only to one location. Then one day, I saw how we were limiting our effectiveness. If I could equip those 100 people, they could go to *100* locations and do what we were doing in just one venue. Why wouldn't I want to empower those 100 people so that each one could be a person empowered to change another person's life wherever they went?

That thinking is part of what I am calling *The Kingdom Mind*. I had a vision to make that happen and I have loved that vision ever since. That's what I began to do. I stopped hosting the event-based programs that were often only attended by people who were already Christians. Those events didn't appeal to the people who did not have a relationship with God. We wanted those who knew the Lord to go and influence people who didn't know Him and bring them to church. That may be a cousin, another relative, a coworker, or a community volunteer. I released them from my program to go and share the message with others.

The church can't embrace this role without the leaders understanding that they are there to ensure that the big picture of the church is implemented in any given location. It will require a shift to *The Kingdom Mind* for pastors to change their perception of how they use their people and how valuable those people are in carrying out the mission and potential of the church.

Then those same leaders will have to help the people in the church think differently about why they are there and what they are to do with what they hear and see. The pastor must then understand that he or she is there to support the people, not perform for the people or drive them to build a bigger church. The pastor is there not to do the work of the ministry, but to equip those who are there for the work of their ministry. That's going to require *The Kingdom Mind*, but Paul gave us the vision for how it should look in Ephesians 4:11-16:

> So Christ himself gave the apostles, the prophets, the evangelists, the pastors and teachers, to equip his people for works of service, so that the body of Christ may be built up until we all reach unity in the faith and in the knowledge of the Son of God and become mature, attaining to the whole measure of the fullness of Christ.

> Then we will no longer be infants, tossed back and forth by the waves, and blown here and there by every wind of teaching and by the cunning and craftiness of people in their deceitful scheming. Instead, speaking the truth in love, we will grow to become in every respect the mature body of him who is the head, that is, Christ. From him the whole body, joined and held together by every supporting ligament, grows and builds itself up in love, as each part does its work.

Let's move on and discuss more about how we can empower the people in the pews in the next chapter.

KINGDOM MIND THOUGHTS

1. Event-driven programs do not equip the people sitting in the pews. Church leaders must engage them in a more personal way.

2. Church growth is not the responsibility of the leaders; discipleship is their responsibility and out of that, God brings the growth.

3. People must be taught the principles of the Kingdom so they have *The Kingdom Mind* that will empower them to "perform" on their stage.

4. The goal of discipleship is faith in Christ, nor conformity to church rules.

CHAPTER 10
WHAT'S IN YOUR HAND?

When I was youth leader years ago, I didn't receive much training as a leader. I had to wing it and was pretty much on my own. I pursued skills and techniques that I thought were going to help me be better at what I wanted to do. My bishop and oversight did not have to worry about what I was doing because I was pursuing knowledge that would help me be more effective at what they had released me to do. I was not building my kingdom, I was building God's kingdom.

You may ask what kinds of skills I sought. Were they spiritual skills? More Bible knowledge or a theological degree? My answer is no, they were not spiritual skills but practical management and leadership skills. I searched out how to manage people. For example, I learned how to maximize business meetings. I learned Robert's Rules of Order because it was the ministry business and board meetings that gave a voice to the membership. I was communicating that it was not my ministry; it was ours and the people had a voice. I also felt that a meeting involved a lot of investment when you considered people's time, so I definitely wanted to make sure those meetings were worthwhile. It is something I still do today.

In Section One, we looked at the story in Exodus 4 when the Lord told Moses to throw down his staff and it turned into a snake, then back into a staff. The Lord demonstrated to Moses that He would be true to His word and empower Moses to perform on the stage God had assigned him. It was also another way of showing Moses that he could use what was in his hand to achieve the will of God so long as he obeyed the Lord.

When Moses lived in Egypt and became aware of his purpose to deliver his people, he had a sword in his hand, and he used that sword to kill an Egyptian. Forty years later, the Lord was speaking to him from the burning bush, and perhaps Moses was thinking, "I can't fight any more. I can't wield a sword." The Lord was telling Moses that he didn't need a sword, military might, or an army. All Moses needed was what was already in his hand, so long as the Lord went with Moses to empower him.

THE HAVES AND HAVE-NOTS

Like Moses, we must learn how to use what is in our hand that initially we don't believe is sufficient for the task at hand. In most cases, that involves learning to utilize the people God has given to us. If we love the vision, we will invest in the people because we need many others, just like Moses needed Aaron, to complement our weaknesses as leaders. This is another area of ministry that requires *The Kingdom Mind*.

As leaders attempt to empower others, I'm finding that the people who don't have the skills are often the ones who are going to volunteer. The people with the skills may not volunteer as often because they don't have the time. The skilled person may be a bank vice president or own an insurance company, or have some other significant leadership role. They may not have the time, but they do have the skill set. This is where *The Kingdom Mind* once again must come into play. The leader must learn to take the skilled or gifted people and utilize them according to whatever time they have available. If they can give an hour a week, then the leader should use it to benefit somebody else's life for that hour, or use the time to benefit people in the congregation who need the information the skilled person possesses.

I'm an inner-city pastor, and people come to my church who don't have jobs or are underemployed, or who are single mothers – or both. Others come who are unmarried fathers with children who don't have a viable income. I need to know how to engage them all. I should not discount any of them because they can't come to church as often or can't lead a ministry, or because they have special challenges or needs.

I want to take another person who has a skill set and use those skills to benefit the single moms, the single dads, and the unemployed in the congregation who need what that successful person has. I am involving the people to do the work of practical ministry and not relying on services or events to magically equip them to do or be what they cannot do or be when they first come to the church. That's also what I call *The Kingdom Mind*.

If we love the vision, we will do this, but it's hard work. We must motivate both groups, the haves and have nots, to be involved. Many people have come from other churches where they grew accustomed to sitting and watching, unless it was to do some typical church task like ushering or nursery work. This requires a different way of thinking that will lead to a different way of doing church.

MORE THAN USHERS

As I explained above, I used to complain that the people I needed to do the work in the ministry did not have the time. I had to learn to train those who had the time and not overlook them. I had to train leaders rather than be content to have people watch me. A church cannot grow without developing and training leaders. If we don't grow leaders, our churches may grow numerically but we will not grow to the point that we are efficiently taking care of our congregations because we don't involve enough people. I hope you see that if you love the vision God has given you, you must deploy other people or the vision will remain in its infancy, regardless of how large your ministry gift may be.

Many of those people who don't have the time can play a part in the process of growing leaders. They don't have to lead a ministry that focuses on leadership growth and development, but they can participate in the teaching and equipping process. *The Kingdom Mind* learns how to use all the people who are in the church by finding out what their skill sets are, and then allowing them to participate in the development of the congregation sitting in the pew so those pew sitters can go into the world and empower others.

Therefore, we need to go back to basics that will require us to transform the thinking of the church, which means transforming the thinking of the leaders. Leaders develop and shape the culture of any church, and that culture should be a Kingdom culture and not one of the denomination or the area in which the church is located. I've got to make sure that as a leader I'm doing all I can to ensure that the people in the pews are rising to the level needed to fulfill the church's mission.

Here is another example of what I am talking about. Many churches develop an effective ushering ministry. It's relatively easy to do and people will usually volunteer for that, since they are coming to church anyway and it gives them a role to play. Others have had church ushers in their family for generations and they take the role quite seriously, actually telling people who inquire of their ministry that they are a church usher.

What's the focus of those ushering efforts? It's usually on how well the ushers greet and seat people. I maintain that there should be more than that to an effective ushering ministry. The ushers are volunteers but someone in leadership must see that person as more than an usher. They are also a father or a son, a mother or a wife. They are grandparents or accountants, daycare workers or consultants. They are retired or traveling for their companies. In other words, they are a potential resource for more than ushering.

I should not only talk to them about how well they are ushering, I should talk to them about their lives, holistically and practically. I need to know how they are doing financially. How are they doing in their families as husbands and wives? I can recommend other training or perhaps another ministry in which they can give an hour or two. All those issues are important because that is how I can disciple the people in the church and empower them to serve in another capacity beyond the Sunday service. When people are being empowered outside of Sunday, then the church impacts its community because it's reaching beyond the walls of the church building.

KINGDOM CHARACTER

Sometimes leaders put themselves on a pedestal, or the people put them there, and they become gods to the people instead of shepherds leading the people. Our goal is to shepherd and lead, not to be worshiped. I don't want anyone worshiping me for I am not God and don't want anyone to treat me like I am. That's the reason I'm reluctant for people to celebrate me because I do not want them to lose sight of who is over our lives, my own included. We as leaders must be so comfortable and secure in who we are that we don't need all that.

What is to my benefit is that I know I am called to do what I do and I do it because I love God and the vision. That must be something that I pass on to the people. I lead in a way that gives them a sense of understanding of what Paul wrote in Philippians 2:5-8 (KJV):

> Let this mind be in you which was also in Christ Jesus, who, being in the form of God, thought it not robbery to be equal with God but made himself of no reputation and became obedient unto death, even the death of the cross.

What is described in those verses is called humility and we as leaders need it in abundance.

The Kingdom is what's important, not we the leaders. We saw earlier that Jesus told Nicodemus that except a man be born again, he cannot see the Kingdom. If it's God's kingdom, then it's the reign, the rule, and the government of God, or commonly called a theocracy – God is at the head. We operate in a culture that is a democracy, but we understand that the purpose of our theocracy is to be a light to the democracy. The democracy may never become a theocracy, because if we think our democracy should become a theocracy, then we must ask why Jesus didn't turn the Roman Empire into a theocracy. Jesus said to render to Caesar [government officials] what belongs to him and to God what belongs to Him (see Matthew 22:21).

The disciples asked Jesus, "Lord, are you at this time going to restore the kingdom to Israel?" (Acts 1:6). Jesus responded that it was not for them to know the times and seasons that only the Father knew. He told them that they shall receive power and were to operate in that Kingdom power while living in the midst of the Roman Empire. Today, we must represent God's kingdom and be light to the democracy, not trying to turn the church into a democracy.

The culture we are in may never change, and we can't start thinking that it's going to change. Our goal is to be light in the realm of the world that we live in, like Lot in Sodom, Daniel in Babylon, or Joseph in Egypt. When Nehemiah was surrounded by all his enemies, he continued his work in spite of their intimidation and ridicule. We are to be a beam of light that allows people to see what it's like when people surrender to the reign, rule and government of God in speech and behavior. When our light shines, people will see what it is like to be a Kingdom citizen as we function in our sphere or on our stage. As a Kingdom citizen, I need to recognize that my life is a representation of the Kingdom. My life *is* the Kingdom from my perspective so that when I'm in this world, I need to allow my light to shine.

Where am I going with this line of thinking? I am saying that character matters in the Kingdom and if we love the vision, we will not undermine it by behavior that is not consistent with Kingdom values or directives. Many leaders, not all, have forgotten what I am referring to as Kingdom character. When we ignore developing a Kingdom character, we give license to everyone we lead to replicate our non-Kingdom character. That's why it's important for us to have Kingdom character.

Paul wrote, "Follow my example, as I follow the example of Christ" (1 Corinthians 11:1). He was putting his life up as a Kingdom model to follow. Paul was saying they were not just following him as a leader, but as a man who was a *doulos* or servant of Jesus Christ. Jesus gave Paul his identity when Jesus became Paul's Master. As Paul followed his Master, he wanted others to follow him. That's *The Kingdom Mind*.

Followers must understand that character is paramount. We must be careful not to derail people in their journey because of our character. Therefore, leaders must tell themselves that what they are doing as an ethical, Kingdom leader is not just their job. Being people of character is who we are on the inside, not who we are in public. I want to be the believer who is a good representative of the kingdom of God, representing Jesus well.

If anything can destroy the voice of the Kingdom, it's leadership who has character that does not represent the standards of the Kingdom. If anything is going to destroy the church community, it will emanate from poor character. If we don't have *The Kingdom Mind* about character, there are no boundaries on language or what gets posted to Facebook or Twitter. People begin to think that's the norm and if people think that's the norm when it's diametrically opposed to everything Jesus taught and modeled, there will be trouble.

In Section One, we learned that we must love God if we are going to lead effectively and promote a godly vision. In this section, we looked at our need to love the vision that God gives us. That means we love the work that goes with the vision and that involves empowering the people in the pews, both the experienced and the novice, the educated and the ignorant, the busy and the not-so-busy.

Loving the vision also means upholding the vision with righteous behavior and integrity. This integrity is not just in money or sexual matters, but it is also in how we utilize and care for the people beyond what we think they can do to help us build the church. In the next section, we will look at the next step we must take after loving God and loving the vision, and that is loving the people.

KINGDOM MIND THOUGHTS

1. Leaders must learn to utilize people who have experience and skills, but little time to help disciple and train those with time but little skill or experience.

2. If leaders love the vision, they will populate the vision with people who can help it come to pass.

3. The Kingdom is not a democracy. *The Kingdom Mind* serves the Lord and not prevailing culture.

4. Kingdom character is not simply a professional duty, it is a Kingdom mandate.

SECTION THREE
LOVE THE PEOPLE

CHAPTER 11
THE KINGDOM REVISITED

We discussed the kingdom of God in Chapter Two, but let's return to that topic once again. The Kingdom is the grace and favor of God that have come to the earth. As a citizen of the Kingdom, I am empowered by God to do and be what I cannot do and be without His help. I sometimes refer to the Kingdom as the Supreme Court because the kingdom of God has power over principalities, powers, and spiritual forces in heavenly places.

There are many other things that Jesus and the apostles said about the Kingdom, too many to mention them all here. Of interest is the series of parables found in Matthew 13. There Jesus presented a few similes describing what the Kingdom of heaven is like, rather than what the church is like (Matthew was a Jew and Jews did not like to use God's name lest they misuse it; thus his reference to the Kingdom of heaven rather than the Kingdom of God).

In Matthew 13, Jesus taught about the Kingdom in the parables of the sower, the weeds, the mustard seed and yeast, the pearl and the hidden treasure, and the parable of the net. Jesus began each parable with the words, "the Kingdom of heaven is like." Jesus' focus was on the Kingdom and that should be our focus as well.

The Kingdom was the focus of Jesus' disciples, including Paul and Barnabas, who told the believers in multiple locations, "We must go through many hardships to enter the kingdom of God" (Acts 14:22). Later, Paul wrote to the Romans, "For the kingdom of God is not meat and drink; but righteousness, and peace, and joy in the Holy Ghost" (Romans 14:17 KJV).

The kingdom of God also embodies our core values. Jesus said in Matthew 5:16, "In the same way, let your light shine before others, that they may see your good deeds and glorify your Father in heaven." Then in Matthew 6:33, He added, "But seek first his kingdom and his righteousness, and all these things [the needs of life] will be given to you as well." We are to seek God's way of doing things, God's order, and God's plan.

KINGDOM LOVE

The primary core value and motivation for all we do in the Kingdom is love. As we saw in Section One, we are to love the Lord our God with all our heart, soul, mind, and strength and then love one another as God has loved us. Jesus said, "By this shall all men know that ye are my disciples, if ye have love one to another" (John 13:35 KJV). We love through what we say and what we do. We love, value, and forgive people, which are other expressions of unconditional love.

Our love is not based on whether others do something appealing or favorable for us or not. Love does not have an ethnic, national, or denominational target. It is love for everybody regardless of their behavior, belief system, or culture. Love doesn't mean we always agree with everything people do but we love them because they are human beings and we are supposed to love them.

In the Kingdom, God is transforming us into the kind of people who carry out our life business in partnership with Jesus Christ. We represent Him and not our own interests when we interact with others. Therefore, we learn how to live and act in cooperation with the power of God as we act out our delight in loving and serving God and others: "Delight thyself also in the LORD: AND HE SHALL GIVE THEE THE DESIRES OF THINE HEART" (Psalms 37:4 KJV). The source of the delight is Psalms 1:1 (KJV):

> Blessed is the man that walketh not in the counsel of the ungodly, nor standeth in the way of sinners, nor sitteth in the seat of the scornful. But his delight is in the law of the Lord; and in his law doth he meditate day and night.

We must establish Jesus as Lord of our lives. He cannot be Lord In theory but in all matters such as our speech, behavior, and finances.

OUR CHURCH VISION AND PROGRAMS

We saw earlier that Solomon made a statement in Proverbs 29:18, "Where there is no vision the people perish." It's accurate also to say that where there are no people to run with the vision, the ministry vision stagnates and dies (see Habakkuk 2:2). The only way for a church to fulfill a God-given vision is for individual leaders and members to have the vision for how they can personally contribute toward that vision becoming a reality. It is imperative that leaders take the initiative to describe, disseminate, and then live the vision as we learned in Section Two.

Not too long ago, we debated at the church about the meaning of vision and mission as to which was which. We concluded that the mission would be the shorter statement and the vision would be the longer statement. We had a paragraph for the vision statement and when we finished that exercise, it helped us. It was an adjustment because we didn't usually talk about this in church settings. I was never in a church where people discussed the church's vision and mission statements.

We started out with our mission statement reading, **bringing people's lives into focus with the Word**. Then we adjusted it to "bringing lives into focus with the Word to serve." This helped us build the whole concept that we had to *worship God, connect with others, and serve the world.* That statement summarized our basic approach to ministry, which is to empower people and then send them out.

The fact that our church is an expression of God's kingdom and not just a church that exists in isolation or as part of a select group has caused us to develop ministries that go beyond business-as-usual Sunday services. In addition to the church, we now have a school for kindergarten through the third grade. Before the school, we started a pre-kindergarten, because our thought was that if we were going to educate children from the inner-city, we had to get them as early in life as possible. We also offer our facilities to AAU basketball, soccer, and volleyball. We sponsor after-school and summer programs through our Kids Care department.

We have started two corporations; one is the church corporation and the other called the Human Services Corporation. The Human Service Corporation oversees the schools and then the church operates on its own as a church corporation. We have also recently revised our ministry model from the one we originally used. This new model uses small groups called Empowerment Zones to act as hubs that make our large church seem like a smaller church. Those groups meet based either on their demographics (where they live or age) or on the interests of the group (what they study, what they have in common, or ministry emphasis), all this with elder approval.

Of course, we have our youth programs – preschool, elementary, middle school, and high school – that take place during Sunday services. Then all our outreach in our community is housed under our Human Services Corporation. Our mission programs consist of people we support in missions work in the countries I mentioned earlier.

My wife gives oversight to the counseling ministry, which also includes the premarital counseling. We have found that a lot of difficulties in marriage originated from what the couples didn't know about each other and about married life in general.

They thought they knew one another, but then later mistake a personality issue for a more serious problem. She has introduced personality assessments to help individuals understand themselves, their partners, and how their styles complement or clash with one another. Those assessments helped me become a better leader because I understood those with whom I was working (and my wife).

You may be thinking that I am repeating myself from earlier chapters, and you would be correct. I am also reiterating all this to introduce this Section. We have done this because the Kingdom motivation must be love, so therefore we love people and want to meet their needs. We should not be in love with the ministry, or being public figures, or having a church that is bigger than some or smaller than others. While public services can meet certain needs, they cannot meet them all. We want to make a difference in the community through our willingness to meet people where they live and not just where they worship. We have done that because we love the people and that love emanates from our love for God and then for the vision God gave us.

The next few chapters will discuss why loving the people is so important to ministry success and church growth. We will look once more at some of the things we have already discussed, but will do so this time through the lens of love for people rather than for God or the vision. We are all in the people business, no matter what business we are in, and need to make sure our hearts are in the right place as we function with *The Kingdom Mind* on the stage God has given us.

KINGDOM MIND THOUGHTS

1. Each of us is proclaiming and then extending the kingdom of God through our stage.

2. The Kingdom embodies our values that define how we live and work.

3. Love is the motivating force behind all Kingdom behavior and activity.

4. We empower and include people in carrying out the vision because we love them.

CHAPTER 12
LOVING PEOPLE

We discussed in Section Two the need to include as many people as are needed in our work if we are serious about loving the vision. No matter how gifted and no matter what the vision is, no leader can accomplish much without many other gifted people who are involved in and committed to the work. That need, however, cannot be the only or even the main reason why we involve other people, for if we are deploying people solely for what they can do for us, then we are in danger of using people for our own ends, even if those ends are noble and spiritual.

I have noticed that churches and most businesses are quite careful with how they spend their money. They look for cost-cutting practices and seek to make every dollar go as far as possible. Yet those same organizations waste human talent every day and don't give it a second thought. They misuse or even abuse people, not setting them up for growth or success, all in the name of profit, or building a bigger church, or serving the Lord. While all those are noble objectives, they don't have the people as the primary focus. The people are a means to an end, which is how capitalism has traditionally viewed people; they are a resource necessary for production, but are replaceable and interchangeable. *The Kingdom Mind* does not see people in that light.

THE REASON TO INVOLVE PEOPLE

I am proposing that we involve people not only because they are important to the work, but also because part of our duty is to help develop those people. In a sense, our work, which is the result of the vision that came from our love for God, should be designed to help build and empower the people. Our work gives them a chance to sharpen and hone their skills, and also to learn how faith functions so they can trust the Lord to do more on their own stage.

The reason some churches don't go beyond the vision of having public services is that the leaders are doing all the ministry. They don't have the time or the skills to establish things like schools and counseling programs, so therefore those things don't get started. What's more, some leaders are not comfortable getting input from others, so they restrict the church's growth to what they know to do.

In the process of building a church that loves people, imparting vision and ministering to people can be difficult if we are not acquiring advice while on the journey. When Moses had the problem that he was trying to serve all the people by himself, his father-in-law Jethro gave him some advice about how he could better serve the children of Israel. Let's look at that story:

> The next day Moses took his seat to serve as judge for the people, and they stood around him from morning till evening. When his father-in-law saw all that Moses was doing for the people, he said, "What is this you are doing for the people? Why do you alone sit as judge, while all these people stand around you from morning till evening?" Moses answered him, "Because the people come to me to seek God's will. Whenever they have a dispute, it is brought to me, and I decide between the parties and inform them of

God's decrees and instructions."

Moses' father-in-law replied, "What you are doing is not good. You and these people who come to you will only wear yourselves out. The work is too heavy for you; you cannot handle it alone. Listen now to me and I will give you some advice, and may God be with you. You must be the people's representative before God and bring their disputes to him. Teach them his decrees and instructions, and show them the way they are to live and how they are to behave. But select capable men from all the people—men who fear God, trustworthy men who hate dishonest gain—and appoint them as officials over thousands, hundreds, fifties and tens. Have them serve as judges for the people at all times, but have them bring every difficult case to you; the simple cases they can decide themselves. That will make your load lighter, because they will share it with you. If you do this and God so commands, you will be able to stand the strain, and all these people will go home satisfied" (Exodus 18:13-23).

We see from this passage that Jethro was concerned not for Moses but for the people because Moses was wearing them out by his inability to delegate and involve other people. This also indicates that people have life challenges even after their freedom from the bondage of sin. After their deliverance, the people with Moses had to be served so they could develop and grow. The same is true for our followers in and out of church settings. They need access to leaders who can listen and help them in a spirit of godly service.

Moses was told by Jethro that he needed to identify and appoint chiefs over thousands, hundreds, fifties, and tens. They had to be capable people who would engender trust in the followers and serve their daily needs. They also needed to know that when they encountered something they could not handle, they were to bring it to Moses – they had to know their boundaries and limitations. Once implemented, that suggestion made Moses' life easier and simpler and it did the same for the people.

JOB DESCRIPTIONS

When leaders love the vision and the people, they have job descriptions that create boundaries to facilitate the fulfillment of the vision. These boundaries help the people understand what their roles and responsibilities are, and must be adhered to at all times. These boundaries control the movement of the people like a highway, moving people back and forth toward a goal or destination, whether it is in ministry or in their own personal lives. This is also an expression of the leaders' love for the people, for it gives the people specific tasks and does not allow the people to wander aimlessly.

The leaders who guide people and explain their boundaries do both by stating the purpose – the why, what, the responsibilities in, and the how – of the vision. That is all explained through a job description that identifies what everyone needs to do. The leader presents the big picture or vision, and then everyone's job description lines up with that.

The leader's role is then to ensure that the vision statement is implemented and fulfilled, and the leaders function within their own boundaries to coordinate the human assets that will help realize the vision. It's not the hard assets like buildings or technology that are the most important, but rather the people who are any leader's greatest asset. Therefore, church leaders must invest in the people for the people's welfare so the Kingdom can be furthered.

When the leader mobilizes people and creates a team environment, it becomes a tremendous competitive advantage and asset, and that allows the team to focus on the task with an expectation of success. Everyone is focused on their roles, utilizing the skills they have, which are undergirded by character and fueled by personality. All that creates synergy, where the sum of the parts is greater than their individual sums. With synergy, because each person is functioning in what they do best, we have one plus one plus one equaling ten or twenty! *The Kingdom Mind* understands that it's not the leader's stage, but that leader is orchestrating results that no one can achieve by themselves. With *The Kingdom Mind*, the leader helps everyone know what each team member brings to the table, and does not allow anyone to trespass on what someone else can do exceptionally well and with anointing.

BUILDING TRUST

The best leaders empower their teams to achieve greatness. Leaders must empower people because most leaders don't attract people who have the entire package of necessary gifts or skills. Some people come a little rough around the edges and need to be developed and trained. Those people have the desire, but they don't have the skill set. One of the most important characteristics someone who wants to participate can have a desire to be part of the team and gain new skills. After that, there must be the willingness to learn. Then comes the willingness to follow instructions. If they have those three traits – the desire to grow, the willingness to learn, and the ability to follow instructions – then we can guide them to success. If they don't have those three, it's going to be difficult for them to endure the kind of pressure in ministry that will empower them to fulfill the ultimate outcome of the vision. Also, if they don't have those three traits, it will be difficult for the leader to trust them.

Let me give you an example. Let's say I have a ministry I'm considering for you, but I don't know you that well. You have indicated you are willing to be involved, and you have a resume that shows you have some potential and have accomplished some things. I haven't seen what you can or can't do and for me to trust you, I have to see what you do with an assignment over a period of time. Then I can see if you really have the desire and ability to listen and follow directions. If you do, that gives me an indication that you might be a person I can trust and with whom I can work.

I have made the mistake of putting people in roles or responsibilities because I thought I knew them or because they looked good, only to get the shock of my life when they didn't perform. I made my decision based on my assumption that they were going to do a good job. Then I watched them fail because their interaction with people was poor, or they could not build a team, or effectively interact with others.

Sometimes people were enamored with becoming a leader and they had some gifts, but they did not understand all the aspects necessary for leadership – disciplines like meeting deadlines, working with a diverse group of people, setting goals and objectives, setting up meeting agendas, and managing meetings. If these leaders are not at the skill level required, then the effort is going to stall or stagnate.

If we love the people, we will get involved with the people to help them see their deficiencies. Then we will do what we can to get them help – training, counseling, classes, or degrees – so they can be successful on our stage and move on to their own. We do that not because people are a means to an end but a worthy end in and of themselves. We are here to build people up so they can grow and contribute to the Kingdom.

In the next chapter, we will discuss another step leaders need to take if they love the Lord, the vision, and the people. That is the need for leaders to be authentic, which is more than being gifted or skilled, but being transparent and honest with their followers and team members. Let's proceed to that discussion, once we review *The Kingdom Mind* concepts from this chapter.

KINGDOM MIND THOUGHTS

1. Leaders empower people not only so they can be productive to achieve the vision, but also so they can grow and develop as citizens of God's kingdom.

2. People are not a means to an end.

3. Misusing people is an ethical and not just a management or leadership problem.

4. Leaders must create opportunities so people can be proven to be trustworthy by showing they have three traits: the desire to grow, the willingness to learn and be teachable, and the ability to follow directions.

CHAPTER 13
AUTHENTIC LEADERS

Some leaders I have known are insecure and threatened by people around them who are more talented, skilled, or gifted than they are. It is also common that strong leaders with vision often value their ideas more than everyone else's ideas combined. When some are carrying out a church vision, those leaders can be demanding and impatient, thinking that they must always act with urgency because they are doing the work of the Lord. I have seen leaders dismiss their own mistakes but consider it a major problem when others have made theirs, no matter how small the offense.

It is a major revelation for some leaders that they are not perfect or that they are not the only ones allowed to make mistakes. It is an important realization for others that there are good ideas that reside outside of their own brains in the minds of others. People don't expect their leaders to be perfect, but they do expect them to be real and honest about their own shortcomings and failures, and when they are that honest, they become known as authentic leaders.

THE DARK SIDE

All leaders have a dark side, a part of their personality or past that lurks or hides in the dark or shadows of their being. In psychology, this is also referred to as the shadow side – part of someone's personality that shows itself every now and then, but is obscured and sometimes hard to identify. Jesus' disciple Peter had a dark side, and the problem with a dark side is that it is sometimes evident to others and it makes an appearances in times of stress or pressure to cause problems for the owner and those with whom he or she works or lives.

When Jesus told the disciples that they would all fall away because of Him, Peter told the Lord He was wrong:

> "You will all fall away," Jesus told them, "for it is written, 'I will strike the shepherd, and the sheep will be scattered.' But after I have risen, I will go ahead of you into Galilee." Peter declared, "Even if all fall away, I will not." "Truly I tell you," Jesus answered, "today—yes, tonight—before the rooster crows twice you yourself will disown me three times." But Peter insisted emphatically, "Even if I have to die with you, I will never disown you" (Mark 14:27-30).

Peter overestimated his courage and commitment, and it was evident to Jesus that he was doing that. Peter could not see it and the realization it was there had to be extracted when circumstances brought it to light. Peter's failure qualified him in Jesus' eyes to open the doors of the Kingdom with the key he had on the day of Pentecost. Most leaders believe that a dark side like Peter had will disqualify the leader when it comes to light, but that was not the case. Peter's failure *qualified* him for leadership because he had an accurate and not inflated (or lower) evaluation of who he was as a man and disciple.

I described some of the changes I had to make to my leadership style earlier in this book. I came to realize that I had flaws that people saw and caused them problems or pain, but I did not see or properly assess them as flaws. I explained that I had a difficult time expressing gratitude to people who helped me. I didn't know it was necessary to thank them but then somebody would say to me, "Pastor, you never say thank you."

When I did my work, I didn't need to hear a thank you, so I assumed no one else needed to hear that. I was managing everybody by what was important to me. I hadn't learned that everybody was different and I did not understand how important diversity of gifting and personality on a team. I had to learn to value each person according to the gift and personality they had, not the one I had or wanted them to have.

Getting to know people was a challenge for me, but knowing people is an important skill for any leader to learn. Knowing people's personality and how they operate for good or bad will allow the leader to place people in roles where they have a chance to succeed. When they do that, leaders can ascertain the best place for them to help accomplish the overall objective.

ENCOURAGING OPENNESS

We must learn to encourage openness among the people on our teams, and it starts with the leader. If the leader is projecting an air of superiority or perfection, that's a shadow side that needs to be brought into the light. If the leader is the only one who can make a mistake, that's a shadow side that also needs to see the light of day. If the leader is sarcastic or demeaning, that's a shadow side that needs to be confronted and changed. The leader must lead the way not only in vision, but in transparency and authenticity.

On our team, we seek to be transparent and open. We share and talk about what we need to accomplish, about what's gone wrong and what's going right. We talk about what we need from one another, and where we are strong and where we are weak. We need to have those discussions on a regular basis if the leader is going to see the vision fulfilled. Only then can the leader obtain the additional resources to help the people get their jobs done.

What's more, the people will know that they can trust the

leader when the leader is vulnerable and open. Now, if the leader is apologizing and confessing faults every day, then the followers may lose some trust because the leader hasn't faced his or her need for more training and development. If while carrying out the vision, however, the leader comes forth to say, "I messed up," or "You do that better than I. I need to follow you," then the followers will be more apt to do the same. It is contagious and the team will benefit from the practice.

My son came to me on one occasion and said, "You know, you're not giving us any leeway. People come talk to you and then whenever they come out of that meeting, they have an idea of where you want them to go. When someone who wasn't with them in your meeting has a different idea, they feel like they have to go back to you to get approval."

I was surprised, but then my son reported that the people attached the phrase, "pastor said" and it was stifling creativity and initiative. I didn't know that empowering people meant giving them the power to make decisions. By not giving them power to make decisions, I was indicating that I didn't trust them. That was a wakeup call for me. I did not have *The Kingdom Mind* that told me these were God's people. I was taking ownership of the people, which I should not have been doing, but I should have been taking ownership of the vision and empowering the people.

Then I discovered that I had another flaw. I had a hard time saying to somebody that their role was no longer needed or the role had grown larger than their gift or skill could oversee. I couldn't tell them that. I kept telling myself they were going to do better, but in reality they were not and could not. When I tried to tell them, I said it so nicely that they didn't hear what I was actually saying. It took me a while to learn that when I did that, I was not really loving or serving those people. I was protecting myself and that was a shadow side I needed to bring to the light.

TRUST

It took me many years to arrive at the place where I could trust other people to do what I knew I should do, but couldn't do.

That again was a function of my personality. I have a personality that expects to get the job done and I don't care what it takes. If you could not get it done, I would take it over and do it myself. At the same time, I was melancholy, which became dominant whenever I interacted with people, which was causing another problem. I would get quiet, work harder, and not confront or even instruct those around me on how to do a better job. Once I admitted that this was a problem, I saw that I was discouraging the good people around me who wanted to help me. I had to get out of the way and let those good people make the kinds of personnel decisions I could not make.

I had to make those changes if I was serious about loving the people. I assumed that I was to treat other people as I would want to be treated, and that was the problem! I needed to learn to treat other people as *they* wanted to be treated and not as I assumed or insisted they be treated. I had empowered them, invested information in them, revealed my heart in them, so at some point I had to trust them. If they met the character criteria that I required to be a leader, then I had to allow them to move forward and not interfere.

For me, loving the vision meant loving it to the point that I accepted the fact that many other people are vitally important to the accomplishment of that vision. I did not have all the answers or gifts, and I had to release some of my leadership to others. If I loved them, I had to give them opportunities to learn and grow so they would be ready for their stage.

Another function of my personality was that I tended to see what was wrong before I saw what was right. I would look at a project and immediately see a problem, asking why we didn't do this or that correctly. I was always focused on what we didn't do correctly instead of what we did do right. I had to get to the place where we started celebrating the things we did right. We could not focus on everything that was wrong. I began to start conversations with people that focused first on what we were doing properly, which meant learning how to applaud the people and celebrate their accomplishments.

Most of the ministry in any church is carried out by volunteers. They must be viewed as an intricate part of what the church is doing so we don't only celebrate the people who are employed by the church, or only celebrate the leader. The volunteers are often the ones who make everything work for the church and I needed to celebrate every volunteer. I had to love them and not just for the work they did. As I mentioned earlier, I had to learn to talk to the ushers not just about how ushering was going but how they were doing in their various life roles.

Years ago, we had an annual volunteer celebration. It was part of our budget and people enjoyed it because we celebrated people who gave their time, talent, and treasure to the church. A church, at least the church I lead, does not function well without those individuals. Appreciating them gives them a sense of belonging and buy-in, a feeling that the leaders care and think about them, and that their volunteering is appreciated. It goes a long way toward energizing them to continue participating and feeling part of ministry. Loving the people is taking all this into consideration whenever anyone is leading a ministry.

Sometimes we love the idea, and when we love the idea, we're more caught up in the idea and not in all the things involved in making that idea or goal come to fruition. We have to focus on all the people who are making it happen. We must have a constant and consistent philosophy of valuing, celebrating, empowering, and mobilizing them. That gives them a sense that the vision is not the pastor's vision but rather *our* vision. When it becomes *our* vision, then we overcome all kinds of obstacles and climb mountains to get where we are going, and we all look back and marvel. When people buy into the vision, it's a wonderful experience because the leaders are not forcing *anyone* to do *anything*. The people are asking what they can do to help and love is motivator for us all.

We want a church in which people love the ministry and its vision, but where love for people is apparent. We want the people to feel like the vision belongs to them. The pastors must model it, and then instill the same concept into the leaders under them. All the leaders must practice it because it's going to benefit the entire structure of the church. It's a top-down strategy when it comes to passing on this philosophy. When leaders follow this plan, they don't have to worry about how various leaders under them are going to function. There is one vision, message, and agenda, and the love flows.

At the end of the day, the church should benefit all the people and not just the leaders. Our role as leaders is to improve people's lives and give them a new perspective about life in Christ. It's about making them feel that they belong. When we cause them to feel like they belong, it's wonderful.

MY TWO PRACTICES

There are two practices I have developed that are permanent fixtures in my leadership philosophy. First, I'm transparent, especially when I'm dealing with people. If I make a mistake, I explain to people that no leader always makes good decisions and I don't do it right all the time. If I do something and it goes against something I said before, especially with my leaders, I apologize because it's the right thing to do. I also do it because I want them to do it whenever they make a mistake with the people with whom they work. If they're too big to apologize, they are in the wrong place. I'm modeling leadership that shows a pastor can apologize to someone and I expect them to adopt that model.

Second, I discuss the vision and how to implement it with anyone who will listen as often as possible. I may have an idea, but I like to discuss it because I don't think my idea or plan is the only one that should be considered. I have something that I want to accomplish and I'm not going to deviate from that, but I may not know the exact steps to get there. That's why I have people around me who can help me see the steps. I've learned to accept ideas from people and I am peace that I'm not the only one who can think or who has an idea. I don't want yes people around me. I don't want people around me saying, "Well, the pastor said it, so let's do it, even though there's a better way."

If people truly love me, they won't do that. They will offer some rebuttal and share their thoughts. Some people say they don't want to disrespect me as the pastor by disagreeing with me, but they are not dishonoring me if we are all pursuing the same vision. I'm giving them the floor so we can talk and have a conversation. I want to know what's on their minds.

Jesus informed His followers that He was going to Jerusalem to suffer many things at the hands of the chief priests and scribes and the elders. Peter immediately spoke up and tried to correct the Lord. Jesus corrected Peter by saying, "Get behind me, Satan." The impressive thing to me is that Peter felt free enough to talk to Jesus like that, even though his perspective was mistaken. What's more, Jesus was free enough to issue a stern rebuke, which Peter accepted and stayed with the group.

There you have a few thoughts on the importance and practice of loving the people to whom God has joined us as we work to advance the Kingdom. If you notice in this past chapter, I offered several examples of the work I had to do to develop into the leader I am today. All those examples required work, time, and sustained effort toward personal and professional development. In the next and last section, I want to talk to you about loving the work that is required once we love God, love the vision, and love the people. *The Kingdom Mind* is not complete until we embrace that fourth and final love, so let's complete our journey together in the next section.

KINGDOM MIND THOUGHTS

1. If leaders love the people, they will value their involvement and ideas, and see their own imperfections as growth opportunities.

2. Leaders must be honest and transparent with their followers.

3. Leaders empower people by mobilizing them, then allowing them the freedom to do their jobs;

4. Leaders keep the vision before the people and explain how each person fits to minimize frustration and produce clarity.

SECTION FOUR
LOVE THE WORK

CHAPTER 14
THE WORK OF PRAYER

Let's review once again. So far, I have often referred to the concept of the kingdom of God, which I define as the reign, rule, and government of God. We each have a stage, a place where God wants us to carry out His assigned duties in a way that is consistent with Kingdom behavior and character. That understanding occupies *The Kingdom Mind*, which is thinking the thoughts of God as they pertain to Him, the vision, and the people.

I have used the example of Jesus' teaching the disciples to pray to add to our understanding of the Kingdom. Let's look at that teaching in its entirety:

> "And when you pray, do not be like the hypocrites, for they love to pray standing in the synagogues and on the street corners to be seen by others. Truly I tell you, they have received their reward in full. But when you pray, go into your room, close the door and pray to your Father, who is unseen. Then your Father, who sees what is done in secret, will reward you. And when you pray, do not keep on babbling

like pagans, for they think they will be heard because of their many words. Do not be like them, for your Father knows what you need before you ask him.

"This, then, is how you should pray: 'Our Father in heaven, hallowed be your name, your kingdom come, *your will be done, on earth as it is in heaven.* Give us today our daily bread. And forgive us our debts, as we also have forgiven our debtors. And lead us not into temptation, but deliver us from the evil one'" (Matthew 6:5-13, emphasis added).

The kingdom of God is the process whereby the Father's will is done on earth as it is already being done in heaven. Getting to know God's will and doing it in a manner that is pleasing to Him is the process known as discipleship. Discipleship requires effort on the part of the disciple as well as the one doing the discipling. Jesus taught His disciples to pray, so it's important for anyone who is training a disciple of Jesus to teach them to do the same. Prayer is the catalyst to stimulate us to walk by faith and engage the ministry and vision that God is giving to each one of us. Because of its importance, I start off this Section with this chapter titled, "The Work of Prayer."

LEARNING TO PRAY

When I refer to prayer as work, I mean that it requires effort and energy, but I do not mean that prayer is what is referred to as works. Works are the things people do to court and invite God's favor through their own energy or ingenuity. Works signify a system or specific acts that people employ to get God to do what they want Him to do. That is not what I am referring to when I label prayer as work. I am saying, however, that prayer is indeed labor, for there are no shortcuts to an effective prayer life, which is mandatory if everything we have discussed so far is to take place.

When I worked at a bank years ago, I met a gentleman who probably didn't finish the sixth grade. This man believed in the good news described in Acts 2 more than anybody I ever knew.

He believed that signs would follow those who believe, and he believed that to the core of his being. A group of us started meeting for prayer with this man, and he took us on a wonderful prayer journey. We took turns staying at one another's homes where we would pray all night. Then I would go to his house a few times a week at lunchtime, and we would have a time of afternoon prayer.

It's hard to explain the power of prayer. In a sense, prayer is like a Friday high school pep rally. When I was in high school, my school would come to the gym in the afternoon to hold a pep rally for the upcoming football game. The football team became our focus of attention, and we would do all kinds of cheers to get everybody excited and motivated about the game that night. There would be a spokesman from the team who assured us that we were going to run all over our opponent. By the end of the rally, we were emotionally into what we knew was going to be a win for our team.

Prayer is like a pep rally that engages us to do the ministry as God opens Himself up to us in prayer. During these prayer times, we receive thoughts and direction from God. Sometimes we have the feeling that we can conquer the world. Prayer proved to be beneficial to me when I saw it as one of the basic disciplines I needed to have in my life. Prayer helped create in me *The Kingdom Mind* that would enable me to read the Word and see something I hadn't seen before. Prayer would engage me and give me the impetus I needed to do God's will.

I reported in Chapter Three that after a year in prayer, I finally summoned the courage to tell my wife, "I am going to be a youth leader and then hold other positions of leadership in our network of churches." Then later after a vision in prayer, I announced that we were moving to Columbus to start a church. There are many other significant events in my life that were initiated and confirmed by the work of prayer.

THE ROLE OF PRAYER

If we are to walk with the Lord successfully, we need to understand that there are disciplines we need to put into place – and one of them is prayer. Jesus said men ought always to pray and not faint (see Luke 18:1). Jesus set an example for us when He prayed as often as he did, sometimes praying all night. He was modeling the discipline we would need to have direct communication with the Father to fulfill His will. Prayer to me is the means available to help us do God's will. Prayer gives us *The Kingdom Mind.*

Allow me to use another sports metaphor when describing prayer. When a coach properly coaches, he or she gives the team a strategy and lays out how the team is going to attack its opponent offensively and defensively. This information gives the team the confidence that they can go out and conquer their opponent. The team then practices the coach's plan, and the pep rally helps motivates the team so they have the energy and motivation to play the game and execute the plan. After that, they believe there is no way they are going to lose.

Prayer is like that. God floods us with all of heaven and assures us that when we go, we are backed up with all the resources we are going to need to accomplish the job. Doubt never enters our minds. We may encounter something that's difficult, but prayer provides a needed push from the Holy Spirit to keep moving forward in faith. Prayer is what keeps reminding us that we can do something because God is with us.

My petitions to the Lord always go something like this: *Lord, I am Your servant. I want You to use me in any way You desire to use me. That's what I want from You. Use me in any way You want to use me.* I never allow restrictions in my petitions or boundaries to my verbiage. I am always generic and broad in the things I ask God to do for, in, and with me.

For example, I remember when I was preaching at a church in Martin's Ferry, Ohio. I was an evangelist in every sense of the word and was always talking about how God wanted to work through signs, wonders, and miracles. In that church, there was a lady who had been suffering with asthma for years. She came forward and we prayed for her. It was just not my faith, but also my prayer life that caused me to get out of the boat and walk on water, so to speak, to pray for that woman's healing. It was water I didn't know I could walk on, but I was willing to walk on it. I prayed for her and she came back to me years later to report that the asthma never came back.

There were several miracles that took place at that church and people told me I should and could exercise that gift anytime I wanted to. I did not agree with their conclusion. If the Holy Spirit was speaking to me about something, I would act on it. I would not act on something like that without knowing the Holy Spirit wanted me to stretch out in that manner. There were times I was petitioning God, saying, *I want You to use me. I'm not going to tell You how, just use me.*

In another meeting in Michigan, we were praying for the sick one Friday night and a young man came forward who couldn't hear. I stepped out on the water again, and all I knew was that I was supposed to pray for him. I did so, but he left that night still unable to hear. Then the next night, his grandmother came to the meeting with him. She came to us while the service was going on to say that the young man had been out playing. For some reason, she decided to call his name. When she called his name, he ran home to her, reporting that he could hear. When I heard that, I had him go outside and I called him. He came in and said he could hear.

My point is that the Spirit directed me to pray for those people and we saw results. The foundation for those public prayers was my personal prayer life, in which I learned to hear from the Lord concerning His will and direction for my ministry. I was careful not to presume that God wanted to use me like that all the time as I saw fit or according to the needs of those around me.

LEARNING TO PRAY

Prayer answers like I just described propel us into our ministry of the Kingdom and onto our stage. Prayer reveals our hearts and exposes our desperate need for God – His presence and help, and our need for Him to reveal His mind to us. It expresses our need for Him to support us as we endeavor to serve Him. Prayer makes a statement to God about our faith and trust in Him. Because prayer makes that statement, it's almost like clearing the air in our minds as to whether we need Him or not. He honors that prayer communication with His abiding presence, support, and help to carry out the ministry that He has given us to implement.

Sometimes people don't pray because they don't know about the power of prayer or because they've never become acquainted with prayer. I learned about prayer because my mother took me and my two siblings to prayer when we were children. We didn't learn much, but she would pray and we sat there on the bench while she and a few other people were praying.

Sometimes she would get upset with us, and would tell us to get down on our knees, and that is what we would do. We weren't praying, but we would be on our knees. Without understanding it, she was instilling in us a need for prayer. When I saw my Great Aunt Mabel praying three times a day, it made it even clearer that I should pray. Then the man at the bank helped me realize that I was going to pray or I was not going to venture out into my assignment or onto my stage. I had to live up to what I knew.

If God wasn't helping me and ministering to me, my ministry would not work. My petitions were asking God to help and guide me. *I need You to guide me. Help me in all I do. Help me in my marriage. Help me be a good father. I need Your guidance. Put me the right people around me, people I need so I can acquire the wisdom to do some of these things I was not trained to do.*

I didn't always have enough role models for how to become a good parent or husband, so I asked God to put the right people around me. Sometimes I didn't have to get specific about what I needed. There were certain things that happened to me, seemingly out of nowhere, and I see those events today as expressions of God's grace when He worked on my behalf when I couldn't work for myself. Grace is always working in my favor, putting me in the position to know that even praying as I do, the answers are an act of grace. I know it's God working in me both to will and to do His good pleasure (see Philippians 2:12).

Second Corinthians 6:1 warns us not receive the grace of God in vain. I am afraid that some people squander God's grace. They receive God's grace but don't build on it to embrace their stage with a transformed *Kingdom Mind*. Paul wrote about enemies of the cross of Christ in Philippians 3:18-19:

> For, as I have often told you before and now tell you again even with tears, many live as enemies of the cross of Christ. Their destiny is destruction, their god is their stomach, and their glory is in their shame. Their mind is set on earthly things.

Paul was not talking about unbelievers who were enemies of the cross. It seems he was referring to people who had made a profession of faith but then became enemies of the cross, which is really the ultimate symbol of the Kingdom. Those enemies of the cross refused to do anything more with their faith than to trust God for salvation. This is not *The Kingdom Mind*. When He rules and reigns, He governs and directs our lives to be involved in the world through faith ventures on our stage. Prayer is the open line of communication that enables us to stay fresh and relevant on our stage.

KINGDOM MIND THOUGHTS

1. Prayer is work but not works.

2. Prayer is like a pep rally to prepare us for the game of life and for our role on our stage.

3. Our petitions should be general when seeking God's will for our lives.

4. Prayer is listening more than speaking, receiving more than sending.

CHAPTER 15

GRACE

Peter penned these words in his first epistle:

Each of you should use whatever gift you have received to serve others, as *faithful stewards of God's grace in its various forms.* If anyone speaks, they should do so as one who speaks the very words of God. If anyone serves, they should do so with the strength God provides, so that in all things God may be praised through Jesus Christ. To him be the glory and the power for ever and ever. Amen (1 Peter 4:10-11, emphasis added).

The work God has assigned (or as I am referring to it as a stage) is an expression of God's grace, which we began to discuss in the previous chapter. We saw that it is possible to receive God's grace in vain (see 2 Corinthians 6:1), so it seems possible to ignore or reject God's grace in the form of the work He has assigned for us to do.

Grace does not allow us to make excuses or to consider

that some situation or call is off-limits. It does not allow us to surrender when we encounter complicated situations or give in when we face issues that had in the past been difficult for us to handle. Grace enables us to do something we could not do and be something we could not be without God's grace. Therefore, love is the motivation of the Kingdom, but *grace is the power of the Kingdom.*

To help us understand grace, the Bible says, "For we are his workmanship, created in Christ Jesus unto good works, which God hath before ordained that we should walk in them" (Ephesians 2:10 KJV). Since grace saved us, grace also upgrades us so we can to live up to the Kingdom standards and values we learn as we grow in Christ.

That upgrade enables us to move into the ministry God has laid out in advance for us. When that grace is operating, we don't surrender to people's addictions or failures. The grace that operates and works for us will operate and work for them. That is disseminated or carried out by the message of love. If the message of love is not declared and lived, it is impossible for the Kingdom to function. Without grace, the Kingdom would have no effect. The Kingdom can only come through the message of grace and reflection of God's light in our lives. If our lives reflect Him, the kingdom of God is truly at hand for people to see and learn from.

When God's grace is present, we function without measuring our success by numbers, or our acreage, or by who we know, or with whom we are associated. Grace comes specifically because we are connected to Jesus Christ through His love for us: "While we were yet sinners, Christ died for us" (Romans 5:8).

Paul said we have been given the message of reconciliation (see 2 Corinthians 5:18), which is again a part of the Kingdom. That reconciliation message brings man to God through Jesus Christ, who is the human expression of God's love, God's mind and thoughts, and His will. Jesus Christ has now become the bridge between man and God, so that human beings can have a relationship with Him. In our relationship with God, the bridge between us is love and it's there by grace.

When we talk about the Kingdom coming and His will being done on earth as it is in heaven, that is Jesus in action through His people as He carries out the will of Him who sent Him. It becomes the paradigm for us. When the Bible says to let this mind be in us that was also in Christ Jesus (see Philippians 2:5), it was Jesus' mind to do the will of the Father. Jesus said, "My meat is to do the will of him that sent me, and to finish his work" (John 4:34 KJV). Jesus was nourished by doing the will of the Father. The will of the Father so dominated Him that it gave Him a reason to rise in the morning and carry out His mission because it was ingrained in Him to do the will of His Father.

LOVE YOUR STAGE

Jesus was a masterful public speaker and teacher. He utilized His skills as He stood (and still stands) on His stage of purpose on earth. He doesn't tell all people, however, that they need to be public speakers. He doesn't tell every person that they need to be an artist. We are here to do the will of Him who sent us by using the skills that He gave us and we developed. That is part of loving the work He has given us to do. It is this skill that opens the door for me to enter my stage of purpose. When I enter that purpose or performance, it places me in the presence of an audience that He has selected for me to reach.

Once again, you may think this is elementary and not understand where I am going with this train of thought. If your work and gifts are part of God's grace, then why would you want to change, diminish, or even exchange them for another? You may compare yourself to another performer on their stage and think, "I need to be more like that person. I wish I was a better speaker. If only I could sing. I need to get more organized." When we say or think any of those things, we are not loving the work and are actually receiving the grace of God in vain, just as Paul warned us not to do.

God chose your grace package of gifts and assigned your work. When you wish you or your assignment were different, you are saying, "God, You made a mistake. You can't expect me to do this work with my current gifts." Now, there may be skills that you can acquire and develop, but I am talking about the tendency to doubt your capability based on the basic essence of who you are. If you yearn to be in full-time church ministry but you are a medical doctor, you are rejecting your stage in favor of one you *think* is more in line with God's will. That is not loving your work.

I have heard some people say that they wished they could do something for the Lord. By that, they meant they wished they were in ministry like I am. They had a romantic and misguided notion that dates back to the early church that a call to ministry was spiritually superior to any other vocation or line of work. In fact, the word vocation eventually came to be used exclusively for anyone who was called to a ministry in the church.

The opportunity given you to serve others is your stage of purpose. You must see that if you are a nurse, that's the stage God has chosen for you and it's equal to any other stage. It may not reach as many people as someone else's stage, but that doesn't make it inferior in any way. The bottom line if you are a nurse is to understand that this skill set and vocation you have is your chance to fulfill God's purpose and do His will. That's an expression of Kingdom love and that's loving your work. To do your Kingdom work to the best of your ability with the skill set you have is the highest expression of Kingdom love I can think of.

When you are on your stage, you do something that ultimately wins you attention so you can confess who you are. Your union with Christ allows that to take place. If you abide in Him, and He abides with you, there's going to be fruit that comes from that relationship. Through God's grace on the stage provided for you through your skill and with this audience you have, you cannot diminish the importance or the worth of your skill. You must acknowledge that your purpose has value because if you don't, it minimizes your effectiveness on your stage.

DON'T COMPARE YOURSELF TO ANYONE ELSE

Minimizing your skill's value or worth can occur when you

compare what you have to somebody else's skill. I can't compare my skill with your skill or anybody else's for that matter. Once I start comparing my skill and try to rank where it stands in God's eyes, I'm usually comparing the fruit of our labors. If another person is doing or achieving more, does it devalue my skill or purpose? If I'm thinking about numbers and I don't get the kind of response you get, I tend to devalue what I have. Everything we have has value and is meant for a certain place and time. I can't devalue my skills or what I do when I compare them to what others achieve or accomplish.

Let's say you are a janitor. Society may say that where you work or that particular skill has little or no value. That is society's viewpoint but it is not God's. God does not tell us a janitor is better than a doctor or a doctor is better than a bank president. God told Adam that one of his responsibilities as a human being was that he should have dominion (see Genesis 1:28-29). Then He gave him a job description and told him he had to till the land.

If God tells us to clean the rooms or operate on people, our goal is to do the will of Him who sent us, whether we are a janitor or a brain surgeon. Who we are in the eyes of people does not determine our value in our relationship with God. It is not the skill set that's most important, it is the person and his or her obedience to the will of the Father.

What's more, our stage is not about results or prestige, it's about service. Jesus was clear that those who wanted to be great were not to pursue degrees or work that others honored. They were to seek to be servants:

> A dispute also arose among them as to which of them was considered to be greatest. Jesus said to them, "The kings of the Gentiles lord it over them; and those who exercise authority over them call themselves Benefactors. But you are not to be like that. Instead, the greatest among you should be like the youngest, and the one who rules like the one who serves. For who is greater, the one who is at the table or the one who serves? Is it not the one who is

at the table? But I am among you as one who serves (Luke 22:24-27).

Paul later wrote, "But by the grace of God I am what I am, and his grace to me was not without effect. No, I worked harder than all of them—yet not I, but the grace of God that was with me" (1 Corinthians 15:10). Paul had a set of gifts and skills and he accepted them. He did not devalue them because they were not the same as the ones who belonged to anyone else. We must do the same. We are here to do the will of Him who sent us to be a secretary, a football coach, or a lawyer. We cannot minimize of devalue who we are.

We must also remember that God has returns in mind from His investment in us. He holds us accountable for both results and attitudes. If you are a janitor, He wants you to be generous, maybe going beyond what others would normally do as a janitor. You want the company to look the best it ever has. You want the rest rooms to be cleaner so that people will brag about the rest rooms because of the excellence with which they are maintained.

We also cannot allow the failures we have while we are learning to cause us to abandon or dislike the work. For example, I thought my first sermon was going to be a great one. I didn't know what I was doing, but I still thought it was going to be great. The title was "A Great Falling Away," and there was a great falling away as I preached it because it was terrible. I didn't know the Bible, and didn't know much of anything. Nobody responded.

There was another young man my age who also preached in the same service, and this young man did his homework. He was a good preacher, and everyone responded to him and was impressed with his message. Nobody said anything about mine. My point is that I could have devalued my purpose right then and there, saying I wasn't called to preach or teach, but I didn't do that. I knew I could learn to preach if that was what God had for me to do, and I knew it was. The will of the Father is something that automatically comes with the experience of being born again, and His will for me was to preach.

Like Jesus, your purpose is to do the will of Him who sent you. Your character and not just your skill set creates opportunities to fulfill your purpose and to have a relationship with people who are in your sphere of influence. You must have character, purpose, *and* skill, for any one or two without the others is like a three-legged stool that is missing one leg. What's more, you can't be fearful. You can't abort what you have been assigned to do because you are measuring yourself by what the prevailing culture values. Then you will not allow what God is trying to birth in and through you to come forth – you will receive His grace in vain.

God wants people to experience what He's put in you. He wants people to experience not just your skill, but the experiences He has put you through to make you who you are. All that is evident through your stage and is supported by your character so that it is received by people who God wants you to touch and bless. It is not just your mother or your church that you are letting down when you abort your purpose, you are letting Jesus down. Your most important relationship is with Him, and you don't want to let Him down.

So far, we have seen that loving the work involves embracing whatever it is you must do to be successful on your stage. It also entails accepting who you are and not desiring to be someone other than who God made you to be. When you accept who you are, then loving the work involves paying any price needed to develop and grow the gifts and skills God has given you.

As church leaders, we must be careful not to set up a distinction between those who work in and for the church and those who do not. We can easily communicate that those who work in the church are spiritually superior or have superior work, especially those called to preach and pastor. While those are noble callings and activities, they are no better than any other calling. We must support whatever will help people develop, which we will discuss in the next chapter, after we review the thinking of *The Kingdom Mind* from this chapter.

KINGDOM MIND THOUGHTS

1. Loving the work requires that you embrace and not reject the work God has for you in His kingdom.

2. When people compare themselves to others and yearn for another stage or gift, they are telling God He made a mistake when He made them the way He did.

3. Prevailing culture may not value what God values.

4. Purpose, skill, and character are a three-legged stool and all three legs need to be in order or else there will be a problem.

CHAPTER 16
MORE ON GRACE

I relate to the story of Joseph found in Genesis 37-50 for many reasons. One of those reasons is because Joseph had a gift that was not his and for which he did nothing to earn it. Joseph could interpret dreams by the grace of God, and the dream God gave him caused his brothers to be jealous and ultimately to do something terrible to Joseph. Our gifts are just like that. We didn't do anything to earn them; God gave them to us according to His sovereign will:

> To each person the manifestation of the Spirit is given for the benefit of all. For one person is given through the Spirit the message of wisdom, and another the message of knowledge according to the same Spirit, to another faith by the same Spirit, and to another gifts of healing by the one Spirit, to another performance of miracles, to another prophecy, and to another discernment of spirits, to another different kinds of tongues, and to another the interpretation of tongues. It is one and the same Spirit, distributing

as he decides to each person, who produces all these things (1 Corinthians 12:7-11).

We can develop our gifts but that is not the same as earning them. We identify what they are and then we shape our world around their use.

There was no place Joseph went where he didn't prosper, even after his brothers' dastardly deeds. The Bible says that the Lord was with Joseph, and Potiphar, the prison warden, and Pharaoh all recognized that the Lord was with him. He went through many tough times, but God was there and Joseph continued to carry out his purpose on the stage called Egypt.

I attribute that also to the grace of God, for God was doing for him what he could not do for himself. Joseph could not allow himself to lose sight of who or where he was. He could not devalue his skill and his gift in Egypt because he had not chosen to be there; his brothers had sold him into slavery there. He did everything so well that he stood out wherever he was, all because the Lord was with him. What did he do for the Lord to be with him like He was? Joseph did nothing.

Joseph was the son of Jacob and the great grandson of Abraham, both of whom were also products of the grace of God. Abraham was not looking to be the father of a nation, and Jacob was not attempting to father the twelve tribes. God bestowed that purpose stage on both men. Jesus described the grace of God when He said that no man comes to the Father except the Father draws him (see John 6:44). The disciples were picked from among many Jews, most of whom were better candidates. They were not the smartest or most gifted; God chose them by grace. Paul understood that he was also an apostle because of grace:

> Because of this I remind you to rekindle God's gift that you possess through the laying on of my hands. For God did not give us a Spirit of fear but of power and love and self-control. So do not be ashamed of the testimony about our Lord or of me, a prisoner for his sake, but by God's power accept your share

of suffering for the gospel. He is the one who saved us and called us with a holy calling, *not based on our works but on his own purpose and grace, granted to us in Christ Jesus before time began,* but now made visible through the appearing of our Savior Christ Jesus. He has broken the power of death and brought life and immortality to light through the gospel! For this gospel I was appointed a preacher and apostle and teacher (2 Timothy 1:6-11, emphasis added).

I am grateful to the one who has strengthened me, Christ Jesus our Lord, because he considered me faithful in putting me into ministry, even though I was formerly a blasphemer and a persecutor, and an arrogant man. But I was treated with mercy because I acted ignorantly in unbelief, and *our Lord's grace was abundant,* bringing faith and love in Christ Jesus (1 Timothy 1:12-14, emphasis added).

The Church often misunderstands how to respond to gifted or successful people because they misunderstand the role that grace had in their success. We give a lot of credit to people for what they have done in their careers, but what they did is by God's grace. If we don't appreciate God coming to us the way He does, we will take all the credit for what we have done and not give credit to the One who put us in the place to do it.

At the end of Genesis, Joseph told his brothers that they meant him harm and evil, but God meant what they had done for good (see Genesis 50:20). God put Joseph in the right place at the right time to save the world from starvation and to order Israel's steps toward Egypt. I repeat that Joseph did not choose this path or stage; it was chosen for him.

SIGNIFICANT LIVES

Because of God's grace, we must see our lives as more significant than we sometimes consider them to be. At this point, you may be thinking, "Pastor, you are contradicting yourself.

First, you say that we overestimate the value of what people have done. Then you say we don't always recognize the significance of those lives." Let me explain further and you will see that there is no contradiction at all.

If God has chosen to bestow a grace gift or stage, then we are doing what God wants us to do with the gifts He has chosen to give us. How powerful is that! The God of the universe has placed us on stages and promises to be with us, to work through us so we can share His grace with other people. That means that we are ambassadors and representatives of God's kingdom, operating in the power that comes with that Kingdom. That's what I mean that we undervalue our placement and skill set. We need *The Kingdom Mind* if we are to accurately determine the power and importance of our stage.

The success on our stage is not ultimately determined by how many rungs of the corporate ladder we have climbed, or how high we have ascended on our company's organizational chart. It is not dependent on the level of education we have attained. God will use those things, but ultimately our success is determined by God's grace. Therefore, we as leaders should be looking for evidence of God's grace present in someone's life and not only focus on what they have accomplished or the titles the world has given them.

If God has placed you on a stage, you should walk in the confidence of God's gracious choice and not your professional or educational achievements. You should not undervalue God's grace He has shown by placing you somewhere, but should not overvalue your own accomplishments. It's all about God's grace as He structures His kingdom, and your Kingdom thinking needs to be in line with His.

Don't measure your life by how society measures it, for their values are often not consistent with God's values. Measure your life by the fact that God's grace entered your life, which makes a big difference and makes you a significant person. It's not what you do, it's who put His hand on you to bring you to a place to confess Him as Lord. The Father was wooing you, and the moment you accepted His invitation, you became a significant person.

That's the attitude you should carry onto your stage as a doctor, lawyer, janitor, nurse, or pastor. All those roles represent nothing but the grace of God. The grace of God is what we salute when we worship Him. When we get everything in the right perspective and proper order, our lives take on a different measure of value because we understand that it's the grace of God that has put us where we are and given us this new life.

For those of us who are church leaders, we need new ways to think about who we are and the gifts we have. When we stop comparing ourselves and our results to other leaders, we will be free to rejoice in the influence God has given us, even if that influence doesn't translate into numbers. Leaders are not smart enough to orchestrate everything in their world, so they must learn to live with their limitations. At the same time, they can stop undervaluing their stage simply because it isn't as big or seemingly influential as the one down the street or in another state. The same holds true for you no matter what your role or stage is.

Properly valuing who we are in Christ will enable us to love the work, even when the work isn't progressing the way we think it should or the way we would hope it would. In the next chapter, we will revisit a significant hindrance to loving the work and that is the people whom God gives roles or parts to play on our stage. Let's look once again at the need to empower the people as part of this section's theme.

KINGDOM MIND THOUGHTS

1. Joseph had no role in obtaining the gift God gave him. The same is true for our gifts.

2. We must not overestimate our accomplishments. They are the result of God's grace.

3. We must not underestimate the power of being a Kingdom representative wherever our stage venue is located.

4. We are to be people of influence, and our results will vary according to our gift and God's grace.

CHAPTER 17
MORE ON WORKING WITH PEOPLE

In Numbers 20, we read about the incident that cost Moses his opportunity to enter the Promised Land along with the people:

> In the first month the whole Israelite community arrived at the Desert of Zin, and they stayed at Kadesh. There Miriam died and was buried.

> Now there was no water for the community, and the people gathered in opposition to Moses and Aaron. They quarreled with Moses and said, "If only we had died when our brothers fell dead before the Lord! Why did you bring the Lord's community into this wilderness, that we and our livestock should die here? Why did you bring us up out of Egypt to this terrible place? It has no grain or figs, grapevines or pomegranates. And there is no water to drink!"

> Moses and Aaron went from the assembly to the entrance to the tent of meeting and fell facedown, and

the glory of the Lord appeared to them. The Lord said to Moses, "Take the staff, and you and your brother Aaron gather the assembly together. Speak to that rock before their eyes and it will pour out its water. You will bring water out of the rock for the community so they and their livestock can drink."

So Moses took the staff from the Lord's presence, just as he commanded him. He and Aaron gathered the assembly together in front of the rock and Moses said to them, "Listen, you rebels, must we bring you water out of this rock?" Then Moses raised his arm and struck the rock twice with his staff. Water gushed out, and the community and their livestock drank.

But the Lord said to Moses and Aaron, "Because you did not trust in me enough to honor me as holy in the sight of the Israelites, you will not bring this community into the land I give them" These were the waters of Meribah, where the Israelites quarreled with the Lord and where he was proved holy among them (Numbers 20:1-13).

Read this story carefully and you will pick up on why the Lord was angry with Moses. God told Moses to *speak* to the rock and then water would pour forth for the people. Instead of speaking, Moses took the opportunity to express his frustration with the people and *struck* the rock in anger. The water still poured forth, but God was displeased because Moses had misrepresented the Lord. The people thought God was angry but He wasn't. It was Moses' anger that they saw that day.

If we love the work God has given us, we will not do what Moses did and inject ourselves and our feelings into the work or toward the people. I am not implying that leaders or people should never get angry or show emotion. Anger is a legitimate emotion that God gave us to motivate us to action. The problem is not the anger, but it's the wrong actions that stem from the anger.

This is an important lesson for leaders as we embrace *The*

Kingdom Mind. Leaders must obey what God says, but many times our frustration, like it did for Moses, gets us into trouble. Think of how often Israel gave Moses a difficult time as they wandered the Wilderness. It required great patience on the part of Moses to lead and guide them. Leaders must also confront the inability of the people to see the vision and the Kingdom, and if leaders aren't careful, they will prematurely write people off or carry around a lot of anger.

That means that leaders must be consistent and persistent in communicating the message of the vision. They must paint vivid word pictures of the vision and why it is important to achieve. Leaders must help people believe in themselves, but more than that, teach people to believe in God. Perhaps it is better stated that we need to help the people believe in who God made them to be and who they are. We need to help them identify what the Bible says about them and then repeat it again and again. We may get tired of the sound of our own voices, but we must keep saying it. Don't think the people have it after they have heard it once or twice, because they don't.

Loving the work means that we regularly revisit the reasons the work is being performed. We talk about it, find stories that best reflect its meaning, and share testimonies of what success looks like and how people have grown through the work. And as we discussed loving the people in Section Three, we must work to help the people not to disqualify themselves because of their fears or their past.

I know people who have wonderful skills, but their past has been so confusing and dysfunctional that they don't believe they have value. They're basing their present evaluation of their lives on the dysfunction of their past. Those people must see and understand what the Bible says about them being a new creation. The Apostle Paul had a dysfunctional past as he went about to imprison and persecute every Christian he could find. He was present when the deacon Stephen was killed as reported in Acts 10. When we talk about a dysfunctional past, Paul had one, but God met him on the Damascus road even as he continued to wreak havoc on the church.

Paul then wrote that he had to learn how to forget the things that were behind him so he could reach upward to the things that God had for him (see Philippians 3:13-14). Paul had to remember that his past was just that – gone and done. His past could no longer regulate his present, unless he allowed it to do so. Once he accepted the revolutionary change of direction for his life, he could go on with his new life, and pursue his purpose stage that God revealed to him. Paul had *The Kingdom Mind* where the past was concerned.

Many people in the pews are dealing with a dysfunctional past and they struggle with the present. They are dealing with the traditional way church has been done, having come from another church where things were done in the tradition of their denomination or leader. They don't look at society or church through the eyes of God, but instead through the eyes of their tradition.

God instructed us to go into all the world, and if He says we are to go, that means we are capable of going. He will equip us to go, using the five-fold ministry to assist us in that process – and then He will go with us as we go. Today, He deploys pastors and teachers to influence, teach, and inform us so that we are then able to pursue what God has on His mind for our lives.

We cannot pursue our stage with intensity and purpose without information that is centered on Jesus Christ – who He is and what His demands are for us, based on His will for our lives. Our empowerment comes through the teaching of the church's leadership, which must be according to the formula that Peter wrote about: unadulterated with no additives that could end up corrupting people in their approach to becoming a person of influence that God needs them to be (see 1 Peter 2:1-2).

We must also learn and teach others the proper definition of success in life, work, and ministry. For example, most church leaders evaluate success by the attendance and offering numbers. That is our own definition of success or fruit, but it isn't what God considers increase or success. For example, God said to go into all the world and make disciples in Matthew 28:19-20. He didn't say how many disciples we should make. He said go make some. When we come up with a goal to reach 1,000, and then don't make the goal, we feel like we have not succeeded. Is that an accurate conclusion?

Jesus instructed us to go, which begs the question: Did you go? If you went, then you were successful. It's not how many responded, but rather if you took the step. When we set high and lofty goals on our stage without the Holy Spirit, it's just our ego setting those goals and we never achieve them. The goal in this Kingdom directive is to *go*.

The Kingdom directive for the pastor or teacher is to work so that all people may come to the unity of the faith (see Ephesians 4:14-16). That passage did not say that 100% of everyone who hears will respond. The goal is to teach. Did you do that? If you respond that you did, then you were successful. You must set your mind on perfecting what you do but the ultimate success is in God's hands.

If you're a teacher, you want to perfect your teaching skills since that is the tool God is using to empower others. If you do this well and do it from the heart, and not do it in a deceptive way with improper motives, but do it according to the will of the Father, you will be successful because you are doing what God told you to do.

When the numbers or money don't add up as we thought they would, we can assume we have missed the Lord and settle for watching someone else on their stage – and that's what church has too often become. When church consists of people watching someone on their church stage, the watchers tend to diminish or dismiss their stage outside the church as insignificant or inferior, and they stop loving the work God gave them to do.

I'm not implying that we should not learn to do some things better and see more fruit, but we can't measure our success by numbers or the standard by which corporations determine success. Our success is whether we obeyed or not. We must be consistent and persistent as well as diligent to achieve excellence as we develop our skill sets so that we can influence and empower people if they choose to cooperate with God's grace through us.

When a single mother and her five children come to church and she says she can't go back to school because of her children, we should give her new information to help shape the thinking in her *Kingdom Mind*. We must show her that there is a way and God will help her. It may not be easy but she can do it. We must give her and those like her hope. If we don't give them hope, their condition will overwhelm them, and when did Jesus ever allow a condition to overwhelm anyone?

Think of this other story from the gospel of Mark in chapter four when Jesus was asleep in a boat with His disciples. All His disciples were panicking because of the rain, waves, and wind. They thought they were not going to make it because in their eyes the situation was overwhelming. Jesus got up and said, "Peace, be still!" and immediately the storm dissipated. If you're on a journey and He's in the boat with you, you are going to be afraid at one time or another.

That woman with five children has little money and lives in poor conditions, but Jesus is in the boat with her and our job as leaders is to give her hope. It's not about the weather; it's about where she is seated, and if she's in the boat with Jesus, she's in a very good place.

I've been cautioning our people recently against identifying too passionately with famous R&B or hip-hop personalities. I reminded our people that David wrote songs thousands of years ago that people are still quoting and singing. As God's people in His kingdom, instead of being attracted to fads and cultural trends, we should become attractive. We can't be attractive if we don't come to grips with the fact that our meat is to do the will of him who sent us (see John 4:34). We can't be attractive if we don't love our stage and work to maximize our presence on it.

If someone is a song writer and that's their stage, how many lyrics do you think Jesus could give them? What chords could He give them so they don't have to listen to R&B or hip-hop? Look at the chords and lyrics He's given you to sing the song of your life and work. If we don't get musicians and singers to think that way, they will surrender their stage to watch somebody else's stage who could care less about Jesus Christ or His kingdom.

I'm not implying that we would have the best of everything, but we should be advocates for God-inspired music, chords, rhythms, and instruments. We ought to be advocates for worship and not downplay it. If that is your gift, stop dismissing or denigrating it because you haven't made a million dollars from selling your music. God is not keeping track of how many copies you sold. God is looking to see if you took His gift and used it so that you reached your maximum potential. Did you put your everything into it? If you did, you were successful

When I was growing up, there was a lady who lived across from my grandmother. My mother and I would go to my grandmother's house almost every day at 3 PM and that neighbor lady would be singing. We could hear her practicing and giving her voice a workout, and I knew she did not get paid a dime for training the choir or for the work she did with musical groups. She didn't get paid, but she worked to master her skill.

If you are serious about loving your work, you will need to devote effort to master your skills and gifts. I don't see as many people pursuing mastery of skills as I once did. Some take their skills and because they do a little, they think the world owes them something. Our problem is that we either devalue our gift, or we don't exert enough energy and money to master it. How many singers rehearse every day? How many singers sit down and practice and play to no one in particular? How many aren't getting ready for anything specific, but they are playing and praying, asking God for inspiration? I hope you are, for God does not promote people with potential; He promotes people who have developed their potential.

LISTENING

In Chapter Twelve, I mentioned that one of the traits I am looking for in people with whom I work is their willingness and ability to listen to others, and effort to comprehend what they heard. If we love our work, we've must be willing to listen to others. My ability to listen and learn were of great help to me when I started out and they still are. Once I saw its value and learned how to listen, I was able to do much more than what I could do before, things I didn't know how to do. To listen to other people was invaluable because they were telling me I could do what I did not think I could do.

Listening is one of the keys to attain success. When you listen, it indicates that you don't know it all. If someone knew more than I did, I wanted to learn what they knew, so I was willing to sit and listen to them – especially if they were successful. If I don't want to go through all the disciplines after I listen, then that's my fault, but listening is the start that opens the door of *The Kingdom Mind* to learn and develop.

The Kingdom Mind realizes that things haven't changed, that our meat is to do the will of Him who sent us. Our need to have wisdom is never going to change no matter what century we live in. Being taught puts is in a better position to accomplish what we think it is that God wants us to accomplish in and for the Kingdom.

In the next chapter, we will look at creativity and its great enemy, fear. If you are going to love your work, you will have to overcome your fear and be as creative as God wants you to be. Let's move on to look at creativity and fear now.

KINGDOM MIND THOUGHTS

1. Not being able to work with people will eventually undermine the work you love.

2. Listening to others who are successful at what they do and then emulating them is called Kingdom wisdom.

3. You must be serious to master the skills that will lead to your purpose stage performance.

4. Success is defined by your obedience, not by the quantity of the results.

CHAPTER 18
FEAR AND CREATIVITY

Let's start this chapter by looking at what the psalmist wrote in Psalm 1, which we mentioned previously:

> Blessed is the man that walks not in the counsel of the ungodly, nor stands in the way of the sinner, nor sits in the seat of the scornful, but his delight is in the law of the Lord and in that law he meditates day and night. He will be like a tree planted by the rivers of water. That brings forth its fruit in its season. And its leaves shall not wither and whatsoever he does with it shall prosper.

The key statements for me in Psalm 1 are "brings forth fruit in its season" and "its leaves shall not wither."

We are planted by a river, which means that if we are meditating on His word day and night, we are constantly being fed. We are in a place where our tree and fruit are growing and developing and our leaves are not withering. Our fruitfulness does not depend on the weather, for our roots go down deep to draw the sustenance we need. Our fruitfulness on our stage is about where we are planted and not about our work environment, the attitude of those on our team, or the economy.

Since our success is determined by where we are planted, we should develop and grow as if we are always in summer season. The changing seasons will not determine if we succeed or fail, but the determining factor is whether we are planted in a relationship with Jesus Christ. If we are, then the will of the Father is being done on earth as it is in heaven through us. We are radiant with that beam of God's light reflecting off us, even in darkness. The darkness of changing seasons or nighttime are not able to overcome our light.

That light is not our light, it's His. When we are doing His will, that's the light of God dawning through us so others can see that light in our character, our commitment to our purpose, and in the skill set that we value and demonstrate on our stage, whether it is in or out of church. We use all of it to bless and serve others; that's *The Kingdom Mind*. When our leaves are green and our roots go deep, we are creative people because we are created in the image of the Creator. One expression of loving our work is releasing our creativity to solve problems in new, exciting ways.

FEAR

The great enemy of creativity is fear, which can even manifest as an unhealthy fear of the Lord as expressed by the parable in Matthew 25:

> "Again, it will be like a man going on a journey, who called his servants and entrusted his wealth to them. To one he gave five bags of gold, to another two bags, and to another one bag, each according to his ability. Then he went on his journey. The man who had received five bags of gold went at once and put his money to work and gained five bags more. So also, the one with two bags of gold gained two more. But the man who had received one bag went off, dug a hole in the ground and hid his master's money.

"After a long time the master of those servants returned and settled accounts with them. The man who had received five bags of gold brought the other five. 'Master,' he said, 'you entrusted me with five bags of gold. See, I have gained five more.' "His master replied, 'Well done, good and faithful servant! You have been faithful with a few things; I will put you in charge of many things. Come and share your master's happiness!'

"The man with two bags of gold also came. 'Master,' he said, 'you entrusted me with two bags of gold; see, I have gained two more.' "His master replied, 'Well done, good and faithful servant! You have been faithful with a few things; I will put you in charge of many things. Come and share your master's happiness!'

"Then the man who had received one bag of gold came. 'Master,' he said, 'I knew that you are a hard man, harvesting where you have not sown and gathering where you have not scattered seed. So I was afraid and went out and hid your gold in the ground. See, here is what belongs to you.' "His master replied, 'You wicked, lazy servant! So you knew that I harvest where I have not sown and gather where I have not scattered seed? Well then, you should have put my money on deposit with the bankers, so that when I returned I would have received it back with interest.

"'So take the bag of gold from him and give it to the one who has ten bags. For whoever has will be given more, and they will have an abundance. Whoever does not have, even what they have will be taken from them. And throw that worthless servant outside, into the darkness, where there will be weeping and gnashing of teeth'" (Matthew 25:14-30).

The one with the single talent knew his master was a hard man, that the master reaped where he did not sow. Therefore, he brought back to the master the one talent that had been entrusted to him. He didn't want his master to be angry so he played it safe and didn't lose anything. He didn't gain anything but his goal was not to lose or diminish what he had. That's how many people behave toward God because they don't understand that we are created in the image of God. Part of that image is that we are little creators in the image of the big Creator and God wants us to create and produce fruit.

The message in this parable from Matthew is that God expects *increase*. That was God's mandate to Adam and Eve: "Be fruitful and multiply" (Genesis 1:28). He followed up that command with a directive for Adam to be creative when He brought the animals to Adam to name:

> Now the Lord God had formed out of the ground all the wild animals and all the birds in the sky. He brought them to the man to see what he would name them; and whatever the man called each living creature, that was its name. So the man gave names to all the livestock, the birds in the sky and all the wild animals. But for Adam no suitable helper was found (Genesis 2:19-21).

God did not whisper to Adam what he should name the animals. That was a function of Adam's creativity. We are to be creative and bear fruit on our stage with the values and principles that guide all Kingdom citizens.

CREATIVITY

Consider creativity for a moment. It is happening around you every day. Facebook, Twitter, raising kids, and managing your day are just a few common expressions of daily creativity. We don't think about all that being creative, but it is. My mother used to say she could take $5 and make it look like it was $100. That sounds like the story of five loaves and two fish that fed the multitude, which was a creative act.

Creativity is an innate part of our image and how God

made us to function. The psalmist was correct when he stated in Psalm 139 that we are fearfully and wonderfully made. Creativity is characterized by our ability to perceive the world in new ways. Our creativity is the desire and ability to bring to reality what we see through eyes of faith. Creativity actively turns new and imaginative ideas into something tangible.

Since that also describes how vision works, we can say that vision and its fulfillment are part of a magnificent creative process. When we are at peace with our creativity and not paralyzed by fear, we love our work because it is as natural as a lion roaring or a bee making honey. We see something before it is and we make it a reality through our creativity. That means that church should be one of the most creative places on earth, but it's not. Why? It's because we are afraid.

Our stage assignment can also be called our world. On that stage, we have a chance to create something that enhances and transforms the world around us. Thoughts come to us that are larger than our experience would warrant. We have been functioning in one area but then God expands our world to multiple locations. He creates a larger space for us because God has something He wants from us that demands and expects increase.

This larger space God gives us will require creativity to manage. It's larger than we are, and we don't understand why something larger than we are is being presented. I see many people intimidated by new thoughts and ideas. Those thoughts have potential and possibilities, but the people receiving them have no vision or faith to carry out and express that creative idea. They don't have the skill set to make it happen and don't know where to go. No one can make a person pursue an idea, but as leaders who see the potential in those ideas, we must help the people strategize ways to make their dreams a reality. We can't do that the way church is structured right now, so we need *The Kingdom Mind* so we can make some changes.

The common enemy of making any of this happen is fear. It may disguise itself, but it's fear. There's a great deal of fear in the African American community where my stage is located. There are many reasons for this that I will not get into here, but I have seen enough to know that fear is a terrible thing. I often hear people close to me quoting 2 Timothy 1:7, "God hath not given us the spirit of fear; but of power, and of love, and of a sound mind" (KJV). I hear them quote Philippians 4:13, "I can do all things through Him who strengthens me" (NASB).

I wish quoting those verses made them a reality, but unfortunately, it does not. Fear grips our minds and hearts, and we are content to go to church rather than take our place on our stage. I realized one day that fear is not the opposite of courage; fear is the opposite of faith. When we are afraid, we cannot operate in faith, and if we are not in faith, then we are not pleasing God.

Many leaders cannot help their people get free from fear because the leaders are not free. If they were free, they would not be holding on to their people and their vision so tightly. They hold on because they are afraid if they let go, they will lose something. Of course, there is such a thing as healthy fear, for we should fear talking about the Kingdom but not living it. We should be afraid to violate God's commands while pretending to be Kingdom citizens. The unhealthy fears of failure, success, criticism, looking foolish, and poverty, however, just to name a few, work to rob us of our courage to prepare people for their stage.

We are all susceptible to fear, no matter how much faith success we have had in the past. When we moved into our current church building, an older man who lived on the farmland adjacent to our property came to see me with his real estate agent. The real estate person informed me that his client wanted to sell us the 16 acres next to the church for $100,000. All the reasons why we could not purchase the property flooded my mind. We had just taken out a loan on our new building. We couldn't afford it; we didn't have any use for it; what would the people say? All those fears caused me to say no and so we didn't buy it because I was afraid. I regret not buying it to this day.

If we are going to be creative, then we must learn to stare down the fear that entangles us. The problem is not an emotional problem; the problem is how we think. Therefore, we need to learn new ways of thinking if we are going to love our creativity and our work. Let's talk in the next chapter about how we can develop these new ways of thinking.

KINGDOM MIND THOUGHTS

1. We were created in the image of the Creator to be creative.

2. The great enemy of our creativity is fear.

3. Fear is not the opposite of courage, it is the opposite of and the enemy of faith.

4. We will need creativity if we are to be fruitful and successful on our assigned stage.

CHAPTER 19
NEW THOUGHTS

I have discovered that once we step out in faith, our greatest point of vulnerability is right after we have exercised our faith. We are then afraid that we will go too far and ask the Lord for too much. That's why I didn't buy the property that I mentioned at the end of the last chapter. I was afraid right after I had exercised great faith to buy and build.

The church has instilled this kind of fear in people when we have taught them to go and do the will of God, but be careful not to miss or get ahead of the Lord. That causes people to second guess what they are thinking and to wait for more confirmations. When we do that, we instill in them and then reinforce apprehension and fear. The role of the leader in the Kingdom is to coax people into their God-given purpose and do whatever they can do to equip them to be successful. They must go outside their comfort zone and the limitations of their previous experiences, and sometimes the people don't want to go there.

I read an article recently that simply defined creativity as the process of bringing something new into being. Creativity requires passion and commitment. It brings to our awareness what was previously hidden and directs us to new life experiences that emanate from a heightened consciousness of a new potential reality. The moment we see the new before it exists, it can lead to a feeling of ecstasy. When we start counting the cost, however, fear enters in, causing us to lose sight of that ecstasy connected to the revelation. The moment after the new idea or creative thought comes to us, we start counting the cost and conclude that we cannot afford the new.

WHERE DO NEW THOUGHTS COME FROM?

Sometimes we don't give attention to the origination of the new thought or the possibilities of the outcome. Therefore, we never complete the interval between the origination of the thought and the outcome of the idea because we get stuck in the middle. When we understand that the new thought is quite possibly from God and that the new outcome can help many people, those two conclusions should give us the energy to deal with the interval between seeing and doing it. The leader's responsibility is to help people determine where their thought came from and recognize the potential it has to bless others. When people see that, and when leaders see the results in people when they see that, we will all love our work.

People get stuck in their current ruts and in the difficulties of everyday life. They look at their problems and lose all the energy and motivation to do something. It's difficult for me as a leader to see why others don't see the potential and possibilities in their ideas and move forward to get something accomplished. When we face an uphill climb, too often we conclude that it must be the enemy, that's it not the Lord. That mentality relates back to what I said about having faith as a grain of mustard seed and moving mountains. In this case, the mountain is fear and it is inside of us as I described in Chapter Seven.

If we can't conquer our internal mountain, then we can't conquer the new world that God is giving us. All that new world needs is for someone to climb over the internal mountain of their unbelief and fear to discover and experience the world God has created for them. They cannot move into that new world, however, because they are stuck. If people can start facing their fears by admitting they have them, they could be set free from their fear.

When we first started New Covenant Believers' Church, I told the people that God was going to show us through the fulfillment of the corporate dream how our individual dreams will come to pass, because the church started from nothing and became something. It's the same process we need to put in place in our own lives, but people living in fear cannot connect what we did as the church to what they need to do. They believed the pastor was someone special or the other successful people they knew were in a different category than they were, so they allowed fear to stop them before they ever got started.

IMAGINATION AND CREATIVITY

People must learn to use their imaginations to visualize the future as a means to help them overcome fear. God gave Moses a vision and helped him visualize a mobile tabernacle. Later, David used his imagination to design and describe the Temple so he and others could see and build it. I once accompanied a man who restored homes and I had no vision for those houses, but he did. I could not imagine who would want to do anything with those rundown dwellings.

That person who was going to remodel them, however, saw something else. He saw how the end was going to be from the beginning, along with the profit he could make. Even though he saw all that, if he could not act because of his fear of the unknown, even though he had the resources to do the work, he would not even put a bid in on a house. You may have some of the resources to make something you envision happen, but if you are afraid to take that first or second step, you won't find what you need or invest what you have.

When Israel built the mobile tabernacle in the Wilderness, how did they figure out how to apply that gold overlay? God gave someone the creative grace gift to perform that function. When God assigns something, He understands how it is going to come to fruition. He never reveals something without the grace needed to fulfill what He originates. Our faith allows us to step out, confident that we will find the resources and know-how as we go. When we sit back in fear, we can't see what's right in front of us and we miss God's provision.

When we watch television, use a computer, or ride a bus, train, or plane, we are using plastics. When we go to the doctor's office or hospital, or shop at a grocery store, we again are relying on plastics. Where did plastic come from and what is it? Plastics are derived from materials found in nature like natural gas, oil, coal, minerals and plants. The first plastics were made by nature, for the rubber from a rubber tree is plastic. Someone had to learn to harvest that rubber, then someone learned to make synthetic rubber, and then someone developed plastics.

Someone applied creativity, using the basic elements of our existence like water, air, fossil fuels, sun, wind, plants, minerals, elements, and trees. They creatively harnessed the resources God has given us to invent something that we use every day. Creation emanates from the Creator and He has given us wisdom to create just like He created. Hebrews 11:3 tell us, "By faith we understand that the universe was formed at God's command, so that what is seen was not made out of what was visible." We also read what the psalmist wrote in Psalm 8:4-6:

> What is mankind that you are mindful of them, human beings that you care for them? You have made them a little lower than the angels and crowned them with glory and honor. You made them rulers over the works of your hands; you put everything under their feet:

Then we read in Psalm 104:24, "How many are your works, Lord! In wisdom you made them all; the earth is full of your creatures."

God gives wisdom to create, the same wisdom He used

as the Creator. Without Him, what exists could not exist. When we lose sight of the reality of the source of our sustenance, existence, and creativity, we become a god to ourselves and answer to no one but ourselves. What the world worships was made by someone human, but we worship God who is the source of what was made. Through every star, through every blade of grass and through every living soul, the glory of the ever-present God still shines forth.

We are to equip the saints for the work of the ministry, and their ministry is to extend the kingdom of God wherever God chooses to plant them. That means we cannot conduct business as usual and be content to have events, services, and then more events and more services. We must help people overcome their fears and be creative, and that will require us to be more creative than we have been, which will in turn model for the people the creativity they need to express.

We are supposed to be the motivators and help people see that they can be used to expand the Kingdom by influencing other people in their world. That may mean that God wants to take them to another place that they have never been – a new world or stage. We must equip people to say, "Thy will be done on earth as it is" and see it through. Once we start releasing the creativity, we don't know where it's going to take the people – or the church.

I'm not afraid to try new things in ministry. At times, I have abandoned our services where everyone is together in favor of two services, one for the men and one for the women. We know that sometimes men need to be talking about man things in an open forum, and the same is true for women. Sunday is not so sacred that we can't change the format.

On one occasion, I had a gentleman take us through his process of drug addiction on four consecutive Sunday services. We talked about how his story ended happily after he got into drugs in the first place. Another time, we had a Sunday morning service when I talked about the children in childcare and what needed to happen to make sure that they are not overwhelmed by the tsunami of our modern culture. We discussed things like: How do we get our kids trained and developed? What's the best place for them? What schools are the best places for them? What kind of teachers? How do we find out about the schools?

There's nothing sacred for me in a Sunday gathering. It doesn't have to include preaching because we are developing a ministry that is holistic and can address all of life. That's not just about people coming to church to hear preaching. It is talking about marriage if we are married, or school, education, or how to achieve our dreams or parent our children. In this world, we can't believe that preaching is going to do the trick. It doesn't.

FAITH AND IMAGINATION

Faith requires that there is a certain mindset that follows. Faith comes by hearing and hearing by the word, but it also requires thinking. Therefore, we can't be afraid to use our minds, fearful that the activity of our minds is demonic, preventing us from being in the Spirit when I think and come to conclusions. We cannot develop *The Kingdom Mind* if we are afraid of our minds in the first place. God is not looking to override our minds, but to renew them so we can be transformed (see Romans 12:1-2).

Our minds can be instruments of the devil but they are not necessarily or automatically so. Our mind is a God-given tool to be used as we govern and exercise dominion over God's creation. Therefore, we can't downplay the mind's importance. Adam did not name every animal in Genesis 2 without using his mind. Adam did not have a relationship with Eve without his mind. He did not function in the Garden without his mind. His mind was needed because God said that he could eat of every tree in the Garden except the tree of the knowledge of good and evil. He was warned that the day he ate of that tree, he would die. The mind played a role in that whole process, for when the serpent planted a new thought in Eve's mind contrary to the one God had placed there, well, we know what happened.

We must recognize that the mind shapes our lives according to the direction and content of our thoughts. That's not discounting grace or the Holy Spirit, but it does say that our minds are an organ that must be transformed. I often say that I am a new creation, but my mind needs to be transformed and renewed to accommodate the new me that I am. For me to walk according to who I am, my mind must be transformed to be able to do that. What kind of information am I receiving that allows my mind to bring about my transformation?

Philippians 4:8 states, "Finally, brothers and sisters, whatever is true, whatever is noble, whatever is right, whatever is pure, whatever is lovely, whatever is admirable—if anything is excellent or praiseworthy—think about such things." We should concentrate on the things listed in Philippians because it is through focus and concentration that we begin to shape our lives according to the biblical truth in God's word. That truth helps us understand our relationship with Jesus Christ.

Then we shape our lives according to the reality of that relationship and the reality of the word of God. We are able to obtain a new life by hearing the gospel and the good news of the gospel and the wisdom of His word. We allow the divine to enter our thoughts and we are born again. Then we need new life to enter our thinking so we can become what we heard about. We think according to what we hear and then we become and do what we think. That's why we cannot have a day off to think wrong thoughts.

We take a picture of everything we see and store it in our memory banks. We must always remember that we control the entrance of thoughts and ideas. Proverb says we are to guard our mind because it is the source of life (see Proverbs 4:23). Paul warned us in Philippians 4:6-7:

> Do not be anxious about anything, but in every situation, by prayer and petition, with thanksgiving, present your requests to God. And the peace of God, which transcends all understanding, will guard your hearts and your minds in Christ Jesus.

There was a term used years ago that pertained to

computers: garbage in, garbage out. The same is true for our minds! We determine what kind of thought life we are going to have by what we allow to enter our mind. Jesus said that out of the heart and mind proceed evil thoughts, murders, and adulteries, which is why we must guard our minds. How do we build up and equip our minds for success? It's not just by reading a book or the Bible. It's based on what we hear and who we have around us from whom we get advice and gives us wisdom. All that is part of the intake assisting us to frame a new life through our thought process. We're on our way to a new mind when we first believe, but we have many old thought patterns that need to be corrected as we are taught new things and the Spirit helps us assimilate those new things.

All this relates to loving the work God gave us to do. If we love the work, we will do whatever is necessary to be a help and not a hindrance to that work. That is why our creativity is so important and why we need to confront our fears and replace our fear thoughts with thoughts that are conducive to the new life we have in Christ. Only then will we be able to accept our stage with faith. This issue of our thinking that feeds or hinders our creativity on our God-given stage is so important that we will continue this discussion in the next chapter. For now, let's review what we discussed in this one.

KINGDOM MIND THOUGHTS

1. New thoughts can be the gateway to success and innovation; old thoughts hinder our development in God's kingdom.

2. God created you to be creative. It will help you function on your stage.

3. Fear is the common enemy of God's people as they seek to develop and make progress.

4. Leaders must help people identify their fears, which are rooted in their wrong ways of thinking.

CHAPTER 20
CONFESSIONS
OF FAITH

The most accurate report of who we are is what God says about us and not what somebody else says or how they define us. What does God say about us? He says in Psalm 139:14 that we are fearfully and wonderfully made. We can't allow our experiences to diminish the reality of that statement, even if the totality of our life experiences tries to override that truth. If we allow those experiences to blur or mar that truth, we think more about what's happened to us and allow that to define who we are instead of what God our Creator says. We must always go back and remember that we are fearfully and wonderfully made. That's why we must make confessions about the reality of what God thinks about us and not what society, family, work, or associates think and say.

Confessions of who we are in Christ are important for us to make for two reasons. First, they allow us to hear the truth and we know that faith comes by hearing. Second, we tap into the power of the tongue. The Bible says that death and life are in the power of the tongue (see Proverbs 18:21). Our tongues can speak a new world of reality into existence. If we use our tongues to make a confession, and we hear and believe that confession, we are beginning to form a new world in our minds. Even though we have been in a world of negativity that allowed our experiences to define us – a world where we are being hamstrung by our past – our confessions enable us to create a new world based on the reality that God is the One who defines us. Eventually, what God says about us must transcend what we believe about ourselves, or we will attend church and hear great messages, but go home unchanged and un-transformed.

When we talk about our thinking changing, we are actually changing and renewing our belief system. Our belief system houses our memories, ideas, thoughts, images, and experiences from our past that affect our present beliefs. They reside consciously and subconsciously in our minds and surface in many ways, both positively and negatively. That belief system houses our evaluations – the positive, negative, and neutral ways we view our world. Our belief system houses our self-talk, the constant dialogue that goes on in our minds that stems from our memories, evaluations, and perceptions, and often from what we say about ourselves to ourselves.

Did you ever consider the fact that you have a running conversation with yourself? It tells you how bad you feel about you or how bad your life is. It tells you how dumb you are or how brilliant you are. Your perceptions are your own unique way of viewing things. All these are part of your belief system, which is how you evaluate your memories that produces your self-image.

"I AM NOT A LIAR."

To change our process of thinking, we must go through a process to evaluate our behavior when something happens to us. As a personal example, someone once called me a liar. That accusation was hard for me to accept, and I exploded. My kids heard me explode when this person called me a liar. After I cooled down, I went back to rethink what happened. What did I discover when I felt like that? I discovered that calling me a liar was a sensitive issue. My belief system told me that I was *not* a liar and would never lie. A person could call me anything but I never wanted *anyone* to call me a liar. That comment tapped into something I didn't know was there.

Sometimes we don't know what's in us until we have an encounter like that. In that experience, something emerged and surfaced that I didn't even know was there. I had to go through a process to deal with how that got there in the first place. How did I feel when that happened? What did I think? Why was it such a big issue? Ultimately, I had to go back and apologize to the person who accused me and apologize to my children. I had to rethink my view of being called a liar and the appropriate response if that happened.

What did that experience teach me? It showed me that there were things in me that I didn't know were there. I guarantee there are things in each of us that we also don't know about. Leaders must help people find and change those areas of thought, but leaders cannot do that if they haven't done it themselves. Those areas are what I referred to in Chapter 13 as the leader's dark or shadow sides.

We can change our feelings and actions when we fully understand and have new thoughts about the finished work of Jesus Christ. Because of the work of the cross, God is ever-present in our lives. He is constantly with us, and He loves us. The Bible states in Hebrews 12:1-2,

> Therefore, since we are surrounded by such a great cloud of witnesses, let us throw off everything that hinders and the sin that *so easily entangles*. And let us run with perseverance the race marked out for us, fixing our eyes on Jesus, the pioneer and perfecter of faith. For the joy set before him he endured the cross, scorning its shame, and sat down at the right hand of the throne of God (emphasis added).

That weight that so easily entangles us is often our incorrect and sinful thinking. Paul wrote that we must work to take every thought captive so that each one obeys Christ and aligns with the truth in God's word (see 2 Corinthians 10:5). That is a daunting task, but one that bears much fruit and allows us to love our work and see people for who they are in Him and not according to our own bias or prejudice.

BECAUSE OF THE CROSS . . .

When we consider what Jesus accomplished on the cross, we understand why being transformed and renewed in our mind is essential. What Jesus did was against any thought of self-preservation or self-actualization that anyone has ever had. His thinking was not the thinking of a typical human being; He was selfless and a servant as Paul explained to us:

> In your relationships with one another, have the same mindset as Christ Jesus: Who, being in very nature God, did not consider equality with God something to be used to his own advantage; rather, he made himself nothing by taking the very nature of a servant, being made in human likeness. And being found in appearance as a man, he humbled himself by becoming obedient to death—even death on a cross! Therefore God exalted him to the highest place and gave him the name that is above every name, that at the name of Jesus every knee should bow, in heaven and on earth and under the earth, and every tongue acknowledge that Jesus Christ is Lord, to the glory of God the Father (Philippians 2:5-11).

We do not have a choice if we want to renew our minds or not. Oh, we do have a choice and can reject the process, but if we want to live in the Kingdom, we must have *The Kingdom Mind* and that does not come automatically when we give our lives to Christ. For us to live as Kingdom citizens, we must think like Christ and that requires renewed minds. That renewed mind requires discipline and effort to obtain, but it is also an experience that we desperately need because without it, we cannot change our behaviors and live by the standards of the Kingdom. We cannot be selfless like Jesus if we don't change our thinking from thoughts about me to thoughts about God and others. We cannot love God, the vision, the people, or the work without renewed minds.

Because of the cross, others will participate to help in our mind's renewal. Why do I say that? Because before Christ came into our lives, we did not have true fellowship with others. Now, we have a new family and that family helps us see our blind spots along with our potential. The pastor may participate. There may be an Empowerment Zone (small group) member or leader who speaks into us and gives us new ways of thinking. Because of the cross, God's absolute truth found in His word is the standard for our mind's renewal.

Because of the cross, we are able to see life from God's point of view and think God's thoughts. We witness His love for us from His viewpoint. Because of what Jesus did on the cross, the Holy Spirit is assigned to help us and we accept it so our minds can be renewed. Because of the cross, fear no longer holds us hostage, unless we choose to allow it to do so. Because of the cross, we live as winners through Jesus Christ. Because of the cross, we serve Him and others because He first served us. Our thinking must change for the effects of the cross to work in our lives.

Emotion can evoke a physical response to whatever you are experiencing or thinking. If you visualize and think about cutting and then biting into a lemon, your mouth starts to water. You think about the lemon and it activates your body. That's why worry is not an innocent activity. When you think fearful thoughts, it triggers a physical response and if that worry is unchecked, it can lead to illness and disease. Your thinking is important because what you should want to gain in life is a principled lifestyle. That means you live by principles and not by emotions. Your emotions don't govern you, but the principles do.

Proverbs 23:7 states, "For as he thinketh in his heart, so is he" (KJV). If our thoughts are the source of who and what we are, then we need to pay attention to how we think and what we think about. If we don't pay attention to what we think, we are going to produce actions, behaviors, and emotions consistent with the kind of thinking we have always had. Therefore, *The Kingdom Mind* is essential for spiritual renewal and transformation, and right behaviors that are associated with the kingdom of God.

We don't have enough happening in our churches to help people change the way they think. That's why many church people are depressed. They never say, "Ah, I did that right." Even if they've done it over a period of time and it is second nature to them, they still need to say, "I've been a good mother. I'm doing this right." If they don't, they will overlook the things they do well and never bring them up because they have been trained not to do that.

They will then dwell on what they do wrong, and they will keep producing the behaviors and emotions associated with that wrong thinking. They will quote the Bible, but that practice will not benefit them because it cannot change them. Why? Because their thinking remains unchanged. As I stated earlier, there are many people who quote Philippians 4:11, "I can do all things through Christ" who don't do much. Why? It is because they are afraid. They know the right words, but they are not thinking the right thoughts.

Correct thinking is imperative if we are to arrive at the place where we manifest Kingdom behaviors all the time. When we think right, we do right, and it creates a positive emotion, a sense of joy. Let's assume a running back in football is struggling and the coach calls him out. That player will feel emotion, perhaps anger, frustration, or discouragement. The coach retrains the player to think and act differently, and the player does what the coach says and scores a touchdown in the big game. That player is going to feel another emotion, this time joy and a sense of fulfillment and satisfaction that are positive and beneficial. That player will want to repeat that behavior again and again.

I hope you see how this all relates to the topic in this section: Love the work. When you learn to think properly as the King would want you to think, you will not shy away from the work or fear the work required for you to succeed on your life stage. You will attack the work (in a positive sense) and do whatever you need to do to represent the Kingdom well. You will love the people because you love yourself and you will love the vision because you will understand where your life was headed before you entered the Kingdom when you surrendered your life to Christ.

BETWEEN VISION AND FULFILLMENT

When I was a child, we didn't have a lot of toys to play with, not like children do today. When it would rain outside, we had some little boats. We raced those boats by putting them in the water streaming down to the sewer. We were creative and we were happy. We had good ideas even though we didn't have the resources to purchase a lot of things. We made the most of what we had, and we felt a sense of achievement and accomplishment when we did.

My point is that creativity doesn't show up until we are *forced* to be creative. There is a famous saying that necessity is the mother of invention. When we're forced to be creative, we will be surprised by the kind of things we come up with. If we resist or refuse, then we will be content to watch others on their stage and not find our own. We will grow old and be filled with regrets and live to eat with no purpose or motivation.

Fear comes when we live in the uncertainty of the future as we fixate on what we have (or don't have) today, and that creates faith tension. We see the new but don't have it yet and are still living in the old. We must help people learn how to navigate and escape that tension between what they've seen and its fulfillment. Between those two points is a mountain range or a desert and when they start to cross either, they and their character will be tested. All that is to prepare them for the Promised Land ahead.

They must learn to see the interval in between the vision and the fulfillment as part of their growth process that will build faith and prepare them for the next faith adventure. Leaders who have been through that can help those just starting out on the journey. We can tell them that we thought we were going to die, but we didn't. We didn't think we were going to make it, but we did – and they will too.

But if we only offer event-driven programs, then people will stay in their comfort zones, "have church," and go home in the same place they have always been. It will be like a flight simulator, which can take people all over the world, but in reality they are in exactly the same place as when they entered the simulator. People will learn to love church and what it represents – religious duty, peace, the chance to see people they know and like – but they will not learn to love the work God has assigned for them to do.

The challenge today is how to get those lessons out through every means possible because people are not embracing face-to-face encounters as they once did. They are looking to other places for their fellowship, so we must go where there aren't as many church folk, and we aren't always comfortable there. It resembles the circumstances in Babylon when Daniel served there. Daniel had to compete with the necromancers, sorcerers, soothsayers, politicians, and the professional court officials. He had to compete with all of them to get people's attention, but he did it successfully. We need to do the same.

As an aside, we must assume that Daniel loved his work in Babylon even after all he had been through. He had been transported against his will to a new land and culture, given a new name, taught a new language, and forced to "fellowship" with idolatrous heathen. Yet Daniel was concerned about keeping a kosher diet in Babylon after all he had endured – and he was only a teenager.

Later, when he was called on to describe and interpret the king's dream, Daniel had to deliver bad news and tell the king that he was in trouble if the king did not repent. If I had been Daniel, I would have been glad to deliver a bad report to the man who was chiefly responsible for drastically altering my life. Instead, this is what Daniel said: "My lord, if only the dream applied to your enemies and its meaning to your adversaries!" (Daniel 4:19b). Daniel had learned to respect the king and his surroundings, recognizing that Babylon was his assigned stage. Daniel's thinking was different than most everyone else, and that is why God blessed and prospered him in a foreign land, not in the ministry, but in his role in the government.

By now, I hope you know that I love my work. I am on my stage, and I want to make the most of that opportunity in the days I have left. In the Epilogue, I will share with you an expression of my creativity called Kingdom Brand Development Ministries and why it exists.

That brings me to the end of what I believe needs to happen if we are to have *The Kingdom Mind*. That mind does not only pertain to church work, but any stage that God assigns to anyone, which may be in medicine, business, education, or the military. God's goal is not to get everyone to lead a church, but He does want His church leaders to prepare people for their stage and not just recruit people for the pastor's stage.

For that to happen, leaders and followers must love God, love the vision God gives them, love the people with whom they are called to work and serve, and then love the work it will take to make the vision a reality. While my expertise is the church and its leadership, I know these principles apply to any leader in any situation, and I trust you have gleaned something from these pages that will help you no matter what or where your stage is. Before we end, let me share some closing thoughts in the final chapter.

KINGDOM MIND THOUGHTS

1. It is more important to know what God thinks about us than what we think of ourselves.

2. Our confessions are important to help us change our thinking so we can change our behaviors. There is power in our words and thoughts.

3. There is a wide gap between what people see and how it will be accomplished. Leaders must help people bridge and close that gap.

4. Church leaders must adapt their style to accommodate our modern Babylon that competes for people's attention in many ways.

CHAPTER 21
CONCLUDING THOUGHTS

We have covered a lot of ground since we began and I appreciate you making it to the end. We have seen how loving God, loving the vision, loving the people, and loving the work all play an important role in having what I refer to as *The Kingdom Mind*. I will not attempt to review everything we have discussed, but here are some highlights for you to consider as we conclude:

1. Emphasize utilization not accumulation of people.
2. Move from entertainment to mobilization.
3. Shift from being event-based to empowerment.
4. Don't think church, think Kingdom.
5. Focus on making disciples, not just gaining members.
6. Emphasize development not program outcomes.
7. Move away from the Sunday show to a 24/7 approach to ministry and facility design and function.

8. Weed out useless traditions and creatively re-place them.

9. Change the way people think to change the way they act.

Let's look at some summary thoughts for those of you who are aspiring leaders, or who are called to lead outside the church:

1. You are a citizen of the kingdom of God, with all the rights, privileges, and responsibilities thereof.

2. You have a stage, something for you to do that only you can do, something for you to be that only you can be.

3. You will need not only *The Kingdom Mind* to see your stage, but Kingdom behaviors while you function on that stage.

4. You are born to be creative but your fear will cause you to doubt your creativity.

5. You need mentors and coaches who will help you escape the traps of your own thinking.

6. You must learn to value the diversity of gifts in each person. Then you will look to be part of teams or build teams that have a wide variety of skills and talents.

7. God loves you as you are, while transforming you into a better you.

8. Your thinking is the key to your transformation. Learn to think and confess new thoughts and it will lead to new behaviors that will lead to your transformation.

9. *The Kingdom Mind* not only includes Kingdom thoughts but also Kingdom ethics and values. Your misbehavior can cost you the right to serve on your stage.

I know that I now have less days ahead of me than are behind me. I am in the latter years of my ministry work. That is why I want to devote the remainder of my days to equipping leaders to lead in new ways so they can prepare people for their stages in life. I have preached many sermons and I am sure I will preach a few more, but now I want to build a different kind of organization that will be based on function and not on preaching or doctrine. I want to make my skills and wisdom available to others while maintaining my relevance in a new generation and era of church work.

I am asking the Lord to help me love Him more, so I can love His vision, people, and work to accomplish the vision more effectively. I want to be more effective than I have ever been, and that's one reason why I have written this book. I hope you have been inspired and encouraged by what you have read, and I hope you have questions about how this can all come to pass in your role on your stage. If you have questions, I invite you to join yourself to others seeking the same answers so that together we may learn from one another and be better equipped to advance the Kingdom.

As I close, I think of the benediction in the small letter that Jude wrote that appears in the Bible right before Revelation:

> To him who is able to keep you from stumbling and to present you before his glorious presence without fault and with great joy—to the only God our Savior be glory, majesty, power and authority, through Jesus Christ our Lord, before all ages, now and forevermore! Amen.

Amen and thank you for reading!

EPILOGUE
KINGDOM BRAND DEVELOPMENT MINISTRIES

Over the years, I have observed that there is little to no help for leaders in most churches I visit. There are a lot of conferences and seminars where people hear a preacher and then go home. There are many books (and now, mine is one of them) that outline and describe techniques and ministry or leadership approaches that promise results. We can turn on the TV and find numerous church services and religious events.

Through all that, I saw the need for an organization that did not embrace all the pomp and ceremony of bishops and church protocol. I wanted something that did not repeat the pattern we have seen of conferences and events that emphasized preaching and then more preaching. What I wanted was a support ministry that could engage these churches, pastors, and their leadership in a personal and organizational growth program. I wanted them to support one another with information so everyone had the power to establish an impactful church in their community.

That's about as far as I wanted it to go. I wanted to do something that had long-lasting impact and value, and to ensure that leaders could have at their fingertips anything they needed to boost the influence of their church in their city. I wanted to found something that could pass on best practices to those who were in need and interested. I'm not criticizing the other meetings or associations, but I wanted my approach to add value and purpose so that individuals or small churches were not lost in the shuffle. I wanted something where people could belong to any other organization they wanted to belong to and still identify with mine.

That's why I founded Kingdom Brand Development Ministries (KBDM), which exists to assist pastors and church leaders. If they are Methodist, Baptist, or Pentecostal, they are welcome in KBDM. I founded KBDM to accomplish two objectives. First, KBDM provides a safe place where they can come to discuss challenges they are encountering and share successes they are enjoying in their ministries. Second, it is a place where they can receive information or find skills to use as part of what they need to do in their congregations. Those skills include things like accounting, church growth strategies, team building, and professional development.

We want the members to have confidence that there is someone in KBDM who has been through what they are facing and then draw on and learn from their experience. Members can visit one another to witness firsthand the projects and programs they are considering for their own areas. As a group, we can determine what we lack and reach out to other groups to supplement our experience and knowledge. These are only a few examples of how KBDM functions. As you can see, the community fosters learning by leveraging the experiences and expertise of everyone in the group.

Below is a list of some of the functions of the Kingdom Brand Development Ministries:

1. Create vital grace relationships through interaction, prayer, and encouragement.

2. Create shared-learning through ongoing periodic teaching from KBDM leaders.

3. Examine KBDM principles and walk out their implications in our ministries.

4. Employ strategies in our local churches through community discussion, experiment, review, and analysis.

5. Provide a confidential community for brainstorming ideas and shared problem-solving.

6. Share and leverage the experiences, successes, and failures of the community.

7. Increase effectiveness by sharing resources, skills, and gifts found within the community.

8. Sponsor intra-community training.

9. Engage in best-practices sharing in the areas of human resources, train the trainer, joint projects, ministry technology and utilization, etc.

10. Create a clearinghouse of documents and data, i.e., training manuals, lesson plans, project and planning templates, church management, ministry management and operation plans, compliance, and liability information.

For example, if a church is trying to set up a board of trustees, understand the role of the trustees, or reconfigure their board of trustees, or if they need help with branding and marketing, we can give them the tools required to do that. If they need to know how to set up their financial books or are in need of an audit, we can help them find an accountant. If they need to know how to set up leadership groups, we can assist them with that. We want to help their churches develop, grow, and be influential wherever they may be – in Columbus or outside the United States.

Our Kingdom Brand Summit is a conference we hold regularly to empower people, but we want Kingdom Brand Development Ministries to be more than an event they attend. We want to communicate with them throughout the year and make sure they have all the information and encouragement they need. We don't want to be a group that meets and doesn't meet again until the next year, and when we meet we have good preaching.

I don't even want to include preaching in our Summit meetings because most of our church leaders know how to preach. It seems that most church events and meetings feature preaching, so people can get their fill of preaching someplace else. What they don't always have is the information they need to go beyond the pulpit. We want to focus on how-to information and practical formation, not just the theory but also provide examples of how to put it into practice. The Summit is set up to help churches become what they need to become in their community. It's a concept of no church being left behind, but we do not promise that if someone comes to a Summit, their church will grow to 1,000 members.

Our goal is to help pastors understand that if they put certain principles in place and shift their thinking from worrying about what they need to do to get their church to grow, they will see their churches grow. While pastors are seeking growth, we want them to consider what they are doing with the small groups they currently have (if they have them). Are they empowering the people they have? Are they so worried about what they *don't* have that they are not paying attention to what they *do* have? Are they taking care of the few people they do have? Who do those few people know and what giftedness do they have that the pastor doesn't know about but needs? If pastors empower that handful of people the way they should, if they think about them from a holistic perspective, it is possible for those few people to go find a few more. Suddenly, that church has doubled in size and the process goes on and on.

Our thinking must shift concerning how we think about discipleship, otherwise pastors will constantly and obsessively think about gaining members instead of gaining disciples. If pastors don't consider their ministry as one that emphasizes discipleship, then they will have people who are happy only being a member. The pastor will be happy because he or she has a lot of members who are under the pastor's reign, but not necessarily the rule and government of God. The principle we must keep in mind is that we are to go and make disciples, not gain members. That's the shift in our thinking that must take place. That's what the Kingdom Brand Development Ministries is about, along with all the things that go along with doing that.

NOT A DENOMINATION

Kingdom Brand Development Ministries is not an effort to create a formal church fellowship or organization. We are committed to collective learning and sharing knowledge, skills, and resources. We commit to regularly connect and interact through prayer and community participation. We walk alongside one another without ego or personal agenda. We help each other to advance the kingdom of God. We seek to engage in what we call community practice, which is a group of people or practitioners all involved in a common discipline.

The common discipline refers to the concept of providing useful perspective and a discussion of strategies that provide information to help shape a pastor's thinking. It is our community's objective to engage in the process of collective life learning and shared success of our human endeavor for God. The community functions within KBDM, and the Summit gathering is part of that effort. These communities and connections are members engaged in joint activities and discussions. The members of the KBDM are persons who are actively engaged in a discipline or profession. They develop a common repertoire of resources, experiences, shared stories, tools, and ways of addressing recurring problems in a shared practice.

The KBDM communities develop through a variety of activities such as problem-solving, brainstorming, and requests for information where leaders ask, "Has anyone dealt with the member in this situation?" or "How can we reach youth in our area?" The members can coordinate on purchasing and share information on common strategies. We can share documentation on projects and initiatives so we don't have to repeat the same process if someone has already done something. It is in this spirit that we extend an invitation for others to join us in this connected community of ministry leaders sharing in and encouraging one another to live and build confident, committed, and connected ministries on their assigned stage.

HOW TO OBTAIN MORE INFORMATION ABOUT KBDM

www.kbd-ministries.org

614.475.1678

kbsconnect1@gmail.com

www.ingramcontent.com/pod-product-compliance
Lightning Source LLC
Chambersburg PA
CBHW070039100426
42740CB00013B/2729

ROMANS 12:2 TELLS US PERSONAL TRANSFORMATION COMES THROUGH THE RENEWING OF THE MIND, AND THE BUSINESS OF THE MIND IS THINKING. THEREFORE, TO BE TRANSFORMED, YOU MUST THINK NEW THOUGHTS - THE THOUGHTS OF GOD.

In his third book, Bishop Howard Tillman shares the secrets of personal transformation and his passion to see leaders and their institutions changed through what he describes as *The Kingdom Mind*. This book will help you understand that:

- God has assigned you a stage;
- The church should be discipleship-driven and not event-driven;
- Your ministry and work are to be motivated by your love for God, which will then cause you to love the vision, the people, and the work.

Bishop Tillman's leadership lessons are sure to benefit you, whether you are a seasoned pastor or a young leader just beginning your leadership journey. There is only one way to resist the pressures of modern culture and that is to develop your *Kingdom Mind*. This book will help you do that.

Bishop Howard Tillman has traveled the world preaching the gospel of Jesus Christ. After founding the End-Time Revival Evangelistic Crusade and serving as the chief evangelist, he founded New Covenant Believers' Church in Columbus, Ohio where he still serves as lead pastor. Most recently, he founded Kingdom Brand Development Ministries to equip churches and leaders for successful 21st-century ministry.

urbanpress

ISBN 978-1-63360-090-4

5 1 9 9 9 >

9 781633 600904

$19.99   €16.99   £14.99